Transforming
Anxiety

The HeartMath® Solution for Overcoming Fear and Worry and Creating Serenity

Doc Childre • Deborah Rozman, Ph.D.

New Harbinger Publications, Inc.

Publisher's Note

HeartMath, Heart Lock-In, and Cut-Thru are registered trademarks of the Institute of HeartMath. Freeze-Framer is a registered trademark of Quantum Intech, Inc. Notice and Ease, Power of Neutral, and Attitude Breathing are registered trademarks of Doc Childre.

Distributed in Canada by Raincoast Books

Copyright © 2006 by Doc Childre and Deborah Rozman, Ph.D.
New Harbinger Publications, Inc.
5674 Shattuck Avenue
Oakland, CA 94609
www.newharbinger.com

Cover design by Amy Shoup; Text design by Michele Waters;
Acquired by Catharine Sutker; Edited by Amy Scott

All Rights Reserved. Printed in the United States of America.

Library of Congress Cataloging-in-Publication Data

Childre, Doc Lew, 1945-
   Transforming anxiety : the HeartMath solution for overcoming fear and worry and creating serenity / Doc Childre and Deborah Rozman.
       p. cm.
   ISBN-13: 978-1-57224-444-3
   ISBN-10: 1-57224-444-5
   1. Anxiety—Popular works. 2. Fear—Popular works. 3. Worry. 4. Heart beat—Psychological aspects. I. Rozman, Deborah. II. Title.
   BF575.A6.C63 2006
   152.4'6—dc22

                       2006002533

10   09   08

10   9   8   7   6   5   4

I recommend HeartMath without reservation to all individuals and organizations that are striving to create with the compassion and intelligence of the heart.

—Gary Zukav, author of *The Seat of the Soul* and *The Dancing Wu Li Masters*

Doc Childre and Deborah Rozman have developed a very usable and effective approach to anxiety that is grounded in research, as well as an accumulation of treatment based experience. Their techniques are strategically laid out to build one upon another and can be extremely helpful to people with a variety of anxiety problems.

—Stephen I. Sideroff, PhD, clinical psychologist; assistant professor in the Department of Psychiatry and Biobehavioral Sciences at the University of California, Los Angeles

Transforming Anxiety *is a powerful guide to using positive emotions and loving kindness to reduce anxiety in its myriad of forms. Drawing on both science and common sense, the HeartMath tools will be helpful to anyone when practiced as taught in this straight-forward and easy-to-read book.*

—Frederic Luskin, Ph.D., director of the Stanford Forgiveness Project and author *Forgive for Good*

As a caregiver to cancer patients, I know how essential emotional management is to the healing process. This book offers hope to those who struggle with anxiety and healing to those who put its principles into action. If you let this book into your heart, you will live a happier, healthier and, I believe, longer life.

—Rev. Dr. Michael Barry, director of pastoral care for the Cancer Treatment Centers of America, Eastern Regional Medical Center, in Philadelphia, PA

The power and genius of HeartMath's solution for transforming anxiety is found in its simplicity. The proven techniques shared in this book can be practiced anytime, anywhere, by anyone, and I am confident they will not only transform your anxiety but also transform your life.

> —Jon Gordon, America's #1 energy coach and author of *The 10-Minute Energy Solution*

HeartMath offers individuals of all ages effective strategies to cope with the increasing stress and anxiety of everyday life, and therefore the opportunity to make wiser, less emotionally charged decisions for themselves. Nearly everyone can benefit by using the HeartMath processes to manage the perpetual stresses each of us encounters. This book offers professionals and laypeople alike additional tools to improve their own quality of life and that of their patients and clients.

> —Lilli Friedland, Ph.D., ABPP, member of the Council of Representatives of the American Psychological Association, and past president of the APA's Division 46, Media Psychology

Once again the masters of the heart and mind connection have developed brave new inroads into the realm of humankind. It is no wonder that we continue to see magic from their insights. HeartMath is an unending guide to the inner self, the evolutionary brain and the enigmatic heart. My own experiences with HeartMath continue to underscore their unique approach to health and well-being. Outstanding self-directed knowledge, provided by their new approach to anxiety, not only serves to create better individuals and leaders, but ultimately better companies.

> —Cathy L. Greenberg, Ph.D., physical anthropologist; cofounder and managing partner of h2c (Happy Companies, Healthy People); and coauthor of *What Happy Companies Know*.

The well-being and health benefits that can accrue when people apply the techniques developed by HeartMath can have a significant positive impact on often-incapacitating symptoms associated with anxiety and related syndromes. HeartMath techniques can have an impact on the biological mechanisms that underpin these conditions not only in individuals but groups of individuals in an organization. In my experience, HeartMath is an immensely powerful set of tools, as individuals with anxiety can learn to recognize and modify their own response, reducing the negative affect that anxiety and anxiety-induced symptoms can have on their well-being and overall health.

—Tony Yardley-Jones, FFOM, FRCS, Ph.D., DipMedAc, director of West Berkshire Occupational Health at Royal Berkshire Hospital in Reading, UK

This latest work from HeartMath is a model for other self-help books. The reader is actually taught easy-to-use strategies that can resolve anxiety and other problems in living. HeartMath strategies can be learned and used without professional assistance or they can be taught by practitioners whose goal is to empower their clients. The case studies give the reader hope and confidence. I teach HeartMath concepts in many countries and have found them highly effective with people of widely diverse cultural, geographic, and religious characteristics. HeartMath methods produce healing whether used by themselves or in conjunction with the friendly biofeedback devices famously pioneered by the HeartMath team, which is to say that I have found them to work as well on an isolated tsunami-ravaged beach as in a comfortable clinic. I strongly recommend this book both to individuals seeking to treat themselves, and to their teachers.

—John Hartung, Psy.D., clinical psychologist and teacher at the Colorado School of Professional Psychology, and coauthor of *Energy Psychology and EMDR*

Transforming Anxiety is a unique work of compassionate science. The reader will discover, within its pages, heartfelt empathy whose genesis is founded in some of the most intriguing research of our time. It is an operator's manual for anyone who has ever been caught in the wake of the emotional tsunami known as anxiety. But it is so much more for those who take its wisdom to heart. It is a road map to inner peace and a greater sense of fulfillment.

> —Dan Baker, Ph.D., founding director of the Life Enhancement Center at Canyon Ranch and adjunct faculty member at the University of Arizona, College of Medicine

I called HeartMath to ask them to help after Hurricane Katrina — and they did. We have been using HeartMath techniques with the evacuees with great results. Our clients are pleased and so are we with the effectiveness HeartMath brings into our clinical practice. I am familiar with most of the HeartMath literature, and in my opinion, Transforming Anxiety *is the best book put out by HeartMath to date. It conceptualizes the HeartMath philosophy and combines practical tools, science, and examples in a coherent blend of simplicity that makes it understandable for the layperson and provocatively insightful for the clinician. It has stirred my mind and my heart!*

> —Butch Robicheaux, LCSW, clinical director of Family Services of Baton Rouge, LA

Transforming Anxiety *is a fantastic and functional read for anyone who wishes to bring more balance and alignment into their life. This book gives you the most practical guidance on how to manage your emotional energy. It helps to identify the very nature of anxiety, fear, and the internal loops we create, so that we can truly understand how best to evolve from them.*

> —Kansas Carradine, star of *Cavalia*, the Equestrian Cirque du Soleil

Dedication

Transforming Anxiety is dedicated to the millions of people experiencing increasing levels of worry and anxiety in these rapidly changing times. Anxiety is an understandable response to change and uncertainty, but it can be progressively managed and transformed. From the power of your own heart's intent, you can learn to diminish anxiety reactions as they happen and rebalance your system more quickly after anxiety overload. And, with practice, you can increasingly prevent getting overloaded, especially by some of the same old situations.

At the pace that stress is increasing in the world, neither technology nor other people will be able to free you from anxiety and stress, because it's an individual, inside job. Often people try to practice less stressful attitudes but are still overcome by the weight of a situation. Our intent is to make it easier for you to light a new fire in your commitments to stick with less stressful attitudes and responses to life's challenges. The power to do so is within the intelligence of your own heart, which you already own. Often, to connect with the depth and strength of your heart's intelligence, you need hope. The tools provided in this book are designed to help you build your own hope as you go, which is empowerment in action.

Contents

Acknowledgments

This book is a testimony to the many people who helped research the psychophysiology of anxiety and test the concepts, tools, and techniques provided in this book in their own lives. They have proven, within themselves, the effectiveness of engaging the transformative power of the heart to release worry and resolve anxiety. We especially acknowledge the dedicated staff of HeartMath, who worked with quiet vigilance to help make these methods simple and user-friendly.

We also thank the scientific researchers who are applying the HeartMath findings in their laboratories, as well as the psychologists, psychiatrists, cardiologists, and other health-care professionals now using HeartMath methods in their practices. We appreciate Dr. Jeffrey Stevens for writing the foreword to this book and for his dedicated teaching of HeartMath to anxiety sufferers.

We thank the people who have provided testimonials and transformational stories about their applications of the tools, techniques, and concepts in this book, to help them come alive for others. We wish we had room in the book to share all of their inspiring personal stories. We especially thank those who helped with the planning, editing, and publication of *Transforming Anxiety*: Matt McKay, Catharine Sutker, and others at New Harbinger Publications; Dr. Rollin McCraty, director of research at the Institute of HeartMath; our reference editor, Dana Tomasino, at the Institute of HeartMath; Priscilla Stuckey, our developmental editor; and Amy Scott, our copy editor. Thank you all for your care and commitment to this work.

Foreword

I don't like where I'm going and I don't like where I've been. Why am I in a hurry?

— Bertolt Brecht

What you hold in your hands is an excellent sourcebook of tools developed and perfected by Doc Childre and the Institute of HeartMath. The tools are devoted to the management and transformation of anxiety. This book is, however, much more. Its primary focus is on the development of self-control, stress management, increased objectivity, choices, and compassion.

The quote by Brecht reflects the now all-too-familiar modern sense of perpetual stress. Our physiological systems are better suited to coping with short-term stress. Chronic stress is implicated in numerous psychological and physical maladies, even causing brain damage. The concepts in this book—a blend of the old and new—are a response to the rising tide of perpetual stress.

I first became interested in HeartMath after seeing the institute's research on the health benefits of love. I incorporated HeartMath tools, both personally and professionally, including them in treatment of patients at the Anxiety and Panic Clinic at Kootenai Medical Center, as well as in my private practice. I saw excellent results. With time and further research, there was an increased understanding of why these tools were so effective. It is known that for psychological well-being, an inner locus of control is essential. In contrast, an external locus of control is associated with a sense of being victimized. Anxiety is frequently linked to the perception that "things" — the environment, other people, my feelings, my thoughts — are not in my control.

Feelings and emotions can be difficult to control. As a result, efforts to do so often prove ineffective. Controlling the environment or treating oneself as an object to be manipulated ("Get a grip; don't feel that way!") tends to backfire. "Fighting" anxiety often makes it worse. Arousal patterns — fear, anxiety, anger, panic — impair thinking and judgment while demanding quick action. Bodily sensations in high anxiety states are misinterpreted and catastrophized. Threatening feelings emerging from the brain (the "out of the blue" sensation) can create panic even before any thought occurs.

Emotional regulation or self-regulation with the HeartMath tools fosters a calming of the nervous system through a mixture of physiological and psychological techniques. With practice, these tools increase awareness of a more objective observing "I," helping one to choose to shift attention and create productive feelings like gratitude and appreciation. With practice comes the ability to face and restructure the automatic and ingrained patterns of thoughts and feelings.

The old automatic and trancelike negative patterns tend to grab one's attention. They can, in fact, become one's psychological reality. The mind predicts "Something bad is going to happen," and, as a result, one experiences significant physical and psychological disturbances. This ignores the fact that no one knows what will happen. Likewise, the "what ifs?" are unrecognized as fantasies. The mind has trouble differentiating thoughts and feelings about reality from reality itself. "I'll never eat again" is a real feeling after stuffing oneself. We should, however, be slow to sell the kitchen. The idea that "I would be all right if the world would straighten itself out" is, despite a scarcity of successes, a common and alienating belief.

The idea of reprogramming one's own neurocircuitries is not far-fetched. Indeed, there is a growing body of evidence to support the assertion that changing one's attention and thoughts can and does change the physical structure of the brain itself. The capacity of the brain to alter its structure has been demonstrated, for example, in the treatment of obsessive-compulsive disorder and in the use of cognitive therapy for depression. Changing your thoughts and feelings can also change brain activity. Imagining playing the piano produces a PET (positron emission tomography) scan of the brain that is almost identical to the scan of actually playing the piano. Shifting to positive attitudes and feelings produces PET scans of the brain that are almost identical to the scans generated by "real" mood-altering medicine.

Thoughts and feelings are not things, nor is the mind that contains them. Rather, they seem to be, at least in part, processes. The HeartMath tools improve one's awareness of the relationship between thoughts, feelings, and body rather than working on anxiety itself, much as the fabled Zen archer focuses on the relationship of the bow to the arrow rather than on hitting the target. The movement of awareness and choice to the heart (the nous or eye of the soul to the Greeks), and the withdrawal from ineffective and unnerving states of overidentification, overattachment, and overcare will help lead to the transformation of anxiety. I hope the reader will appreciate and utilize the tools elaborated by Doc Childre and Deborah Rozman. These tools are powerful and full of heart.

—Jeffrey Stevens, MD
North Idaho Mental Health Associates
Kootenai Medical Center
Idaho State University
Coeur d' Alene, Idaho

Introduction

It's obvious that anxiety has become rampant in today's fast-paced society. Most people have some anxiety about themselves, their family, and their future. Anxiety about the world's problems—climate changes, terrorism, diseases—is also on the rise. But increasingly, people experience unremitting anxiety that can turn into an anxiety disorder. Why this is occurring and what individuals can do to overcome fear and worry and create more serenity, especially during uncertain times, is the important subject matter of this book. Below are the most common anxiety disorders as well as the most common ways of addressing them to date. As you will see, the HeartMath solution for addressing anxiety differs in important ways from the usual interventions for anxiety. The HeartMath solution is based on new research on how the heart and brain communicate and how people can harness the power of their physiology to regulate their own emotions to expand intuitive perception. As people achieve their own intuitive heart understanding, anxiety begins to release and is replaced by increasing peace and serenity.

Common Anxiety Disorders

Each of the following types of anxiety disorder may range from very mild to a pathological medical condition where sufferers should see a doctor who specializes in the disorder. These conditions can be triggered by a number of factors: genetic predisposition, traumatic stress, environmental conditions, or repetition of stressful thoughts and anxious reactions over time.

Generalized anxiety disorder (GAD) is the most common anxiety disorder. It starts with repetitive, unmanaged thoughts and emotions and becomes GAD when anxious thoughts and feelings are chronic for six or more months. If you have GAD, you may be irritable or edgy, tire easily, find it hard to focus, have muscle tension, or have difficulty relaxing or sleeping. The National Institute of Mental Health reports that the number of people with generalized anxiety disorder has increased dramatically since 1994, and the number of children taking antianxiety and antidepressant drugs is now soaring. For example, in 2002 nearly 6 percent of all boys and girls were taking antidepressants, triple the rate in the period 1994–96.

Obsessive-compulsive disorder (OCD) is when obsessive thoughts or impulses keep intruding into your awareness. This can be very wearing, and if you suffer from OCD you can feel like a victim of these thoughts. Obsessive thoughts lead to compulsive behaviors—repeated rituals performed to try to release the anxiety, like checking doors or windows again and again to make sure they are locked when there is no danger, or washing your hands over and over. Bulimia, anorexia, and cutting (on the rise among teens) are compulsive behaviors people engage in as an attempt to release deep anxiety. According to the Anxiety Disorders Association of

America, about 25 percent of general anxiety disorders result in some type of obsessive or compulsive disorder.

Panic disorder is identified by recurring panic attacks. The heart beats fast, and there may be tension or pain in the chest. The physical sensations of panic attacks can be overwhelming and scary as you feel as if you are losing control. Many with panic disorder also have phobias or irrational fears. They often have undiagnosed cardiac arrhythmias.

Phobia disorder is a fear of panicking or losing control in certain situations, so those situations are avoided. There are many kinds of phobias, but the most common are fear of heights, fear of panicking in an elevator or elsewhere in public, and fear of what others will think of you if you panic.

Post-traumatic stress disorder (PTSD) occurs after a deep emotional shock or traumatic event, such as witnessing extreme violence, experiencing war, or emotional or physical injury that has left you feeling betrayed or violated.

Common Therapies for Anxiety

The most common forms of therapy for anxiety disorders to date have been drug treatments combined with cognitive behavioral therapies (CBT) to help you take a more rational approach toward your thoughts and reactions and better control them. CBT often includes cognitive restructuring therapy, which usually involves role-playing anxiety-provoking scenarios in order to rehearse more rational responses, then intentionally exposing oneself to anxiety-producing situations in real life while applying cognitive restructuring thoughts to the experience.

The cognitive behavioral model operates from the theory that ineffective thoughts cause disturbed emotions and unhealthy behaviors. CBT tries to help people recognize and stop anxiety-triggering thoughts. CBT by definition does not focus primarily on emotions because it assumes emotions always follow thoughts. Thus, by changing your thoughts, you can gain control over your emotions. Cognitive therapies have helped many to manage or reduce anxiety, but for others they have not been effective. Too often CBT does not release or transform the underlying feeling of anxiety.

Most therapies also include breathing, relaxation, visualization, or meditation techniques to help you become more serene. Breathing exercises change the heart rhythm pattern. The heart rhythm pattern tells the brain how the body feels. Some deep breathing exercises signal the brain that the body is more balanced, which is why they can temporarily help to calm you.

Relaxation and meditation techniques help slow down body and mind, which can also decrease stress and anxiety. However, stress and anxiety often return once the effect wears off if the underlying causes aren't addressed.

Visualization techniques can help distract you from anxious feelings and may generate new positive feelings about what is being visualized. Distraction is much healthier than focusing on or being obsessed with anxious attitudes, feelings, and mental processing. But distraction usually only brings temporary relief from anxiety.

More recently, therapists have been using Buddhist mindfulness meditation and practices, which help people detach from their thoughts and add compassion and kindness to their experiences. Some psychologists are researching and developing what they call acceptance and commitment therapy (ACT), which uses Buddhist distancing techniques, called *defusion*, to teach you to accept anxious feelings rather than resist or try to block them. The theory is that by accepting the anxious feelings, those feelings lose their charge and eventually dissipate through lack of attention.

The Limitations of Cognitive Behavioral Therapies

Since the early 1990s, research in the neurosciences has shown how physiological processes can add to stress and anxiety levels. For example, cardiac arrhythmias (irregular beating patterns of the heart) send a chaotic pattern to the brain, which can trigger anxiety or panic attacks. One study of individuals with sudden-onset arrhythmias found that more than two thirds displayed symptoms of panic disorder. Once the arrhythmia was treated, the symptoms disappeared (Lessmeier et al. 1997). It's a good idea for anyone who has panic attacks to be checked by a doctor for a possible arrhythmia.

It's also clear that emotional processes can operate at a much faster speed than thoughts, frequently bypassing the mind's cognitive reasoning process entirely (LeDoux 1996). While emotions, of course, can be triggered by thoughts, many times they arise from unconscious associations. In other words, emotions can arise independently of the cognitive system and can significantly bias or color perception and thinking. For example, if you became ill after eating mayonnaise as a child, just the smell of mayonnaise now can make you nauseous. Or if you were raised to believe that people of a certain race or culture are violent or untrustworthy, then just seeing a person from that culture can trigger fear, even though your rational mind knows better. Furthermore, researchers have found that people make decisions primarily by emotional assessment and only secondarily by cognitive or rational thinking.

Neuroscience has shown that feelings and thoughts are separate yet interacting functions, which communicate via two-way neural connections between the cognitive and emotional centers of the brain. The neural connections from the emotional to the cognitive center are stronger and more numerous than those going from the cognitive to the emotional centers (LeDoux 1996). This helps explain why emotional attitudes and feelings can disrupt thoughts and dominate thinking, and why it's difficult to turn off strong emotions through rational thought alone. It also helps explains why cognitive behavioral therapies do not work for many.

Emotions:
A Pattern-Matching Process

Emotional sensations and experience result from the ongoing interaction between your heart, brain, nervous, and hormonal systems (McCraty 2003). The brain develops familiar patterns of emotional experience and looks for similarities, differences, and relationships between patterns. Dr. Karl Pribram, Professor Emeritus of Psychology and Psychiatry and head of the Neuropsychological Laboratory at Stanford University, was the first to propose that the brain functions as a complex pattern-identification and matching system (Pribram and Melges 1969). In his model of emotions, past experience builds a set of familiar patterns, which become imprinted in your neural architecture. Patterns of rhythmic activity within the body also provide input to the brain. This input forms the backdrop of emotional experience. These patterns include the heart's rhythmic beating pattern; respiratory, digestive, and hormonal rhythms; and patterns of muscular tension, particularly facial expressions. The brain continuously monitors these inputs in order to help organize perception, cognition, feeling, and behavior. Recurring patterns form a reference pattern against which input patterns are compared. When the brain finds a pattern that matches the reference pattern, it processes the experience as familiar, and it then triggers thoughts, feelings, and physical responses to reinforce the familiar—*even if the pattern is dysfunctional.* This is called a maladapted pattern. For example, if you worry a lot, then worrying can become so familiar to your body that when you're not worrying or anxious you feel uncomfortable. Once worry or anxiety becomes the familiar reference pattern, the brain keeps defaulting to anxious feelings and thoughts as the path of least resistance. This is how habits are formed. The brain considers the familiar to be more comfortable, no matter how irrational it may be. The brain automatically strives to maintain a match with mental, emotional, and physical anxiety responses and habits, despite their detrimental impact on health, well-being, or behavior. Without effective intervention, anxiety can become self-perpetuating and self-reinforcing.

﹩ *Establishing New Patterns*

The way to interrupt this cycle is to introduce dynamic new patterns and to reinforce them until they become familiar, thus establishing a new reference pattern. Once a new reference pattern becomes stabilized, your system will strive to maintain a match with this new baseline (McCraty 2006). This is the goal of most therapies, and this is the goal of HeartMath techniques as well, although the HeartMath model involves a system often overlooked by others: the heart.

The HeartMath Model

Research at the Institute of HeartMath since 1990 has found that the heart plays a primary role in establishing and stabilizing emotional patterns. The heart is a sophisticated information encoding and processing center, with an intrinsic nervous system or "little brain," which enables the heart to learn, remember, and make functional decisions independent of the head brain (Armour 2003; Armour and Kember 2004). The heart rhythm pattern is continually and rapidly modulated by changes in the heart's little brain, which receives information from throughout the body, and by changes in the activity of the autonomic nervous system (ANS). With each beat, the heart not only pumps blood, but also continually transmits neurological, hormonal, pressure, and electromagnetic information to the head brain and throughout the body, affecting how you feel and perceive (McCraty and Childre 2004).

HeartMath researchers have found that therapies or interventions to release and transform anxiety are most effective when they intentionally engage the heart's intelligence system. You can go right to the "heart of the matter" by learning to engage with your heart's rhythmic activity. Learning to intentionally change the pattern of your heart's rhythm will change how you feel and perceive (McCraty and Childre 2004; McCraty 2006). In fact, people commonly do this when feeling stress by taking deep breaths to calm down. This effect is why adults instinctively tell children who are stressed or panicked to take a few deep breaths and calm down so they can assess the situation with more balance. Altering the breathing rhythm by taking several slow, deep breaths alters the heart's rhythm, which in turn sends a different pattern to the brain. You can feel calmer and more at ease through deep breathing. But sustaining slow, deep breathing is difficult for more than a minute or two, so most people default back to their familiar emotional pattern, such as anxiety, fairly quickly.

Heart Rhythm Coherence

HeartMath research has shown that the process of creating a sustainable emotional shift can be facilitated by shifting the heart rhythm into a coherent pattern (see chapter 3), where both branches of the ANS, the parasympathetic and sympathetic, become synchronized. The coherent pattern is a smooth, ordered pattern in the heart rhythm, similar to a sine wave. Shifting into this coherent pattern causes increased harmony and synchronization in the interactions between the heart and brain (McCraty et al. 2005). Coherence in the heart rhythm pattern arises naturally during deep, restful sleep. Coherence in the heart rhythm while awake promotes a calm, balanced, yet alert and responsive state of well-being.

The Positive Emotional Shift

HeartMath research has further shown that shifting your attention to the physical area of the heart, combined with generating a sincere heartfelt positive attitude or feeling, is a quick way to create coherence in the heart rhythm pattern (McCraty et al. 2005; Tiller, McCraty, and Atkinson 1996). The brain associates coherence with feelings of ease, security, and well-being, resulting in a "pattern match" with positive emotional experience. This serves to reinforce the positive emotional shift, making it easier to sustain. Generating positive attitudes and emotions, like kindness, compassion, appreciation, or love, even for a few moments, can trigger in the brain a new perceptual mode that brings new insight and understanding about stressful or anxiety-producing issues. Intuitive understanding helps release anxiety.

HeartMath has developed simple, user-friendly, clinically proven techniques based on this research to help people make quick, positive emotional shifts and to sustain them over longer periods until they become the brain's new reference pattern. Through practicing HeartMath techniques, you can add sustained heart rhythm coherence to any self-help or therapeutic process and power up its effectiveness until new baseline patterns become established, which your brain then recognizes as familiar and strives to maintain.

In this way, the HeartMath solution helps not only to release anxiety but also to transform familiar anxiety patterns into new, healthier, baseline patterns. The HeartMath techniques you will learn in this book will help you empower your own emotional restructuring and repatterning so that healthier perceptions, emotions, and attitudes become a more automatic and familiar way of being.

Many health professionals have found that HeartMath research helps explain why and when other therapies they use work or don't work. Using the HeartMath techniques alone or added to other approaches, while not necessarily a cure-all, is effective not only in helping to clear and transform anxiety, depression, and trauma, but in significantly improving people's outlook and qualify of life.

What You Will Learn in This Book

The HeartMath solution has been researched in psycho-physiology laboratories, validated in clinical studies, and practiced by thousands of people who have successfully transformed their anxiety into ease and clarity, creating more serenity in their lives. The HeartMath methods will help you access a power within yourself that's stronger than worry, anxiety, or fear—the power of your own heart. In this book, you will learn how to connect with the power of the heart to create a *pattern interrupt*. The quick Tools in Action (chapter 3) will show you how to change your familiar anxiety response in the moment, as it occurs. The Cut-Thru and Heart Lock-In techniques (chapters 4 and 6) will give you the power you need to change your biochemistry and neural patterning to healthier functioning.

Through practicing these techniques, you will change the energetics in your subconscious, which changes your perceptions of anxiety-provoking thoughts or situations and changes your beliefs about yourself. You will gain compassion and new intuitive insight about what creates or perpetuates your anxiety. You will look at what you care about and see that care can turn into overidentity or overattachment, creating *overcare*. You will discover how overcare is at the root of most anxiety, and learn to transform overcare back into true care that revitalizes.

It's important that you have a journal or notebook for completing the exercises and worksheets that you will do while reading this book. It's also important to underline or take notes on sections that you want to remember. In this way, you will be able to get the most out of the techniques, as well as keep track of your progress.

This book will not delve into all the various types of anxiety treatments, like other psychological therapies, vitamins, minerals, herbs, nutrition, or physical exercise. There are many, many helpful books available that cover these topics. You can use HeartMath techniques by themselves or add them to any other treatments you find beneficial. As you practice the HeartMath solution, you will also develop heart intuition to draw to you additional remedies that can help.

chapter 1

The Anxiety Epidemic

That the birds of worry and care fly over your head, this you cannot change, but that they build nests in your hair, this you can prevent.

— Ancient Chinese Proverb

"For a long time, my first experience of the day was a tension in my gut," says Matt. "'Learn to relax more,' my doctor advised." Matt had finally decided to talk to his doctor after what seemed like years of waking up feeling like he never went to bed. "As soon as I opened my eyes, I would feel the accumulation of concerns and anxiety about the coming day or difficult people to deal with. Often the discomfort would be because of some uncomfortable conversation I needed to have with someone. No matter how well the day went, the anxious feeling would never completely go away."

Matt is typical of many who suffer from a constant sense of anxiousness and dread. Anxiety like Matt's has become an epidemic. According to the National Institute of Mental Health, one in eight Americans aged eighteen to fifty-four now suffers from an anxiety disorder. One in ten

American women takes antianxiety or antidepressant drugs, and the use of such drugs has nearly tripled in the last decade. While the number isn't quite as high for men, those rates are rising as well.

At the current rate of increase in stress levels, one can expect anxiety statistics to at least double within the next few years. Anxiety is projected to increase not only from work or financial stress, but also from an increase in societal turbulence due to wars, terrorist threats, natural disasters, and the increasing polarization between people of different political parties and religious beliefs.

Anxiety may range in intensity from unease to worry to strong fear. It may last a short while, or it may last a long time, becoming chronic because people don't know how to release it. Undercurrents of anxiety often propel addictive behaviors around alcohol, food, sex, drugs, shopping, or doing anything to extremes. Addictions give temporary relief from obsessive thoughts and feelings. However, underlying the addiction are worrisome thoughts and anxious feelings, often stemming from a lack of self-security or self-worth. People look outside themselves to feel better or safer. Anxiety can make people shun intimacy or, conversely, become overattached and seek a great deal of reassurance from their partners or children. They then feel powerless or out of control, which only reinforces the anxiety. This feeling of lack of control and ongoing anxiety often leads to depression.

Current psychological treatments for anxiety have been ineffective for many. Most therapists try to help people gain objective distance from anxiety-producing thoughts so that they can challenge their underlying beliefs and fears. The theory is that if you change your thoughts and beliefs, then your feelings will change. But this is not always the case.

Feelings and emotions become habitual and often have a life of their own.

The HeartMath solution is different from most treatments in that it addresses emotions directly. HeartMath techniques access the power of your own heart and spirit to change what you couldn't change before. They will help you find the ease and flow through life that you are wanting.

Anxiety Patterns

The problem is that the more you experience anxiety, the more anxiety reactions become etched in your neural circuitry. Anxiety becomes an automatic response to stressful thoughts and feelings. Many people we encounter in our HeartMath programs today report ongoing high- to low-grade anxiety draining their energy. Today's lifestyle has entrained people into constant activity and stress, with too much to do, too much to juggle, and not enough time to do it all. Consequently, the emotional system can't keep up, creating constant emotional oversensitivity and reactivity that contribute to anxiety. Add to that terrorist threats, economic uncertainty, and the fear of disease epidemics, which create an atmosphere of anxiety, and it's understandable why people feel more anxious and edgy.

Anxiety Fatigue

Anxiety keeps the body flooded with stress hormones that drain energy. This is one of the most common reasons for chronic low energy or fatigue. We call it anxiety fatigue. Anxiety fatigue can also make you irritable, impatient, quicker to anger, and more self-judgmental, which often leads to guilt and depression. This cascade of negative emotions creates autonomic nervous system and biochemical imbalances. The autonomic nervous system (ANS) controls 90 percent of the body's involuntary functions. This is one reason why many people with anxiety experience scary physical sensations, including chest tension, shortness of breath, panic attacks, rapid heartbeats, dizziness, sweating, shaking, indigestion, pain in the limbs, insomnia, hormonal or immune system imbalances, and many other symptoms, any of which can make you feel even more anxious or panicked.

If you suffer from any of these physical symptoms, it's critical to see a doctor to have it checked out. Certain physiological conditions, like cardiac arrhythmias, can cause anxiety and panic attacks that go away when the condition is treated.

Stress and Anxiety

If your doctor says your anxiety is stress related, then it's important to understand how your mind and emotions are compounding your symptoms. When you have a strong physical symptom, like panic attacks, your mind and emotions go on the defensive to try to protect you. You can develop a fear of the panic reaction or get caught in the clutches of fear of the fear, which only makes the physical symptoms worse. You can feel like you're going to pass out, have a heart attack, or die, which can be very scary. Ongoing anxiety symptoms often lead to phobias, and you avoid going places or doing things that might cause or worsen a sense of anxiety.

When anxiety becomes a disorder, you can find yourself obsessed by worry and negative or fearful projections, believing your thoughts and images of worst-case scenarios. Anxiety causes negative thoughts to loop around, creating more stress in response, until anxious thoughts and feelings take on a life of their own without needing an event to trigger them. This doesn't make you bad. It's simply a natural consequence of how the body develops patterns. You can use this same patterning process to undo the anxiety.

Beneath the anxiety-provoking thoughts and feelings are your beliefs. Most people have developed some distortions in their beliefs, either through childhood upbringing or from unresolved hurt or shame. For example, you may have a belief that all men are untrustworthy because you were hurt in a relationship, or you may have an unconscious belief that another race or religion is inferior because your parents saw it that way. This is common and only human.

People with anxiety disorders may deny or repress feelings such as frustration or sadness, or even positive feelings like hope and joy. Repressing feelings creates a free-floating anxiety, and you feel anxious without knowing why.

Seeking Help

Unfortunately, it's only when anxiety becomes a serious problem that most people seek help. They read self-help books or go to their doctor to get antianxiety medication or some other therapy. Taking drugs for a period of time to lessen or relieve anxiety, while undergoing counseling to address the underlying causes, has helped many individuals.

Anxiety-reducing drugs may tone down one's symptoms or bring temporary relief (which can be invaluable), but they won't solve the underlying *cause* of anxiety. They also can cause insomnia, lack of sex drive, and other side effects. For some, these side effects are as debilitating as the problem they are designed to help. Tranquilizers, like Valium (diazepam), often prescribed for anxiety, are addictive if taken too often. You need to keep taking more and more to get the same relaxing effect. While drugs may temporarily help relieve anxious or depressed feelings, they also can dull positive feelings and a connection to one's deeper self. For many, that's better than feeling anxious, but it doesn't bring long-term joy or satisfaction in living.

Anxiety can also contribute to other health problems, which people take more drugs to relieve. And then there are the potential side effects of those drugs to be anxious about, like the warnings tagged onto the end of TV commercials, compounding anxiety with anxiety.

The bottom line is that anxiety is spiraling out of control for many. Millions struggle with what to do about anxiety, even if they aren't talking about it. It could be your neighbor, your boss, or even your doctor. Admitting you have anxiety used to be a stigma and many people still fear being judged for it. The bar is being raised and people need to know how to cut through all this. It's time for compassion and action.

Cutting Through Anxiety

In a story about anger, Vicki Smith writes about a Native American grandfather who was talking to his grandson one day. The grandfather said, "I feel as if I have two wolves fighting in my heart. One wolf is the vengeful, angry, violent one. The other is the loving, compassionate one." The grandson asked him, "Which wolf will win the fight in your heart, grandfather?" The grandfather answered, "The one I feed."

Feeding anxiety creates a habit. Once anxiety becomes a habit, it etches a neural pattern that becomes the default reaction. Then you find anxious feelings and thoughts bubbling up automatically as if out of nowhere. Your mind knows better; you conceptually understand that these anxious thoughts and feelings aren't serving you, but you feel like a victim, powerless to change them. Anxiety becomes a closed loop running through your system.

In this day and age, there isn't time to spend years in therapy psychoanalyzing the past, which often only gets you more identified with the past and stuck in the anxiety. The mind and rational thought alone are not strong enough to cut through. You need a power stronger than the mind and emotions. You need the power of your heart.

Research at the Institute of HeartMath has found the most effective way to cut through patterns of anxiety is to connect with the power of your heart to change your physiology and feelings, which then changes your perceptions (McCraty and Childre 2004; McCraty 2006). The HeartMath approach provides you with techniques that help you cut through closed mental and emotional loops and create new patterns in your neural circuitry.

As you practice the HeartMath tools in this book, you develop intuitive intelligence to see what to do. You won't be able to eliminate intrusive thoughts or anxious feelings overnight. Success is correlated with how deeply you experience and believe the new perceptions you gain. Success is also correlated with how much you act on what your heart tells you. As you take responsibility for acting on your new intuitions and insights, you will transform anxiety in your own life and thus contribute to more ease and flow in the lives of those around you as well.

Jeffery Stevens, MD, assistant medical director of the Psychiatric Unit at Kootenai Medical Center in Idaho, comments,

> *I've taught many patients the HeartMath techniques with very good success, especially people with anxiety problems. In one case, an extremely nervous patient*

> *who I've seen for years, but who never responded to multiple psychological and pharmacological interventions, did so well with HeartMath that at first she didn't recognize herself — she was so used to being nervous all the time. She was just delighted. I've had wonderful results using HeartMath with anxiety disorders, phobias, and panic. I have not seen an obvious group of people that can't do it, though persons who have extreme difficulty taking responsibility for their thoughts and feelings can be challenging.*

A Wake-Up Call

People have intuitions that they need to do something, but often don't because they are afraid or feel they don't have time. Transforming anxiety requires taking oneself in hand to make changes and a commitment to see these changes through. It takes individual responsibility and effective tools to transform anxiety into hopeful attitudes and effective action. It's the individual who experiences and bears the burden of anxiety, and it's the individual who has to change it before society will change.

We predict that over the next few years many more people will realize that relieving anxiety is an individual, inside job, and one that is achievable. Overwhelming schedules, health problems, and financial pressures, along with societal upheavals, will take the anxiety epidemic to a whole new level, and people will soon put dealing with emotional stress and anxiety at the top of their to-do lists. It will get less affordable to wait until something serious happens before they seek the help they need.

Transforming anxiety requires a new, serious commitment. Take it on as your own responsibility. Take it on with a new maturity. You can learn how to deal with the pressures of the moment so that stress and anxiety don't accumulate. You can learn to release anxiety as it occurs and find more ease and security inside yourself. Transforming anxiety boils down to taking responsibility for your own feelings. Without gaining a new understanding of your feelings, you won't find ease. It's time to really do something about anxiety. You don't want to keep living this way.

As Donald said,

> *After years of serious anxiety suffering, going from doctors to therapists to alternative treatments with little avail, taking drugs that harmed my health and didn't relieve my anxiety, I finally reached deep inside and connected with my individual responsibility. That's when life lightened up and my anxiety lifted. But I had to follow through with what I knew I needed to do.*

If you don't manage your emotions, then your emotions will manage you. With the HeartMath techniques and tools for accessing your heart power, you *can* transform anxiety. Millions have already used these techniques to transform chronic worry, panic attacks, phobias, post-traumatic stress, and obsessive-compulsive disorders.

To get started, have an honest talk with yourself, and answer the following questions on a piece of paper or in a journal or notebook you keep while you're reading this book and practicing the HeartMath techniques and tools.

🖉 Anxiety Checklist

Describe your type of anxiety the best you can. Check which apply to you.

- o *Ongoing or restless unease*

- o *Chronic worry*

- o *Free-floating anxious or fearful feelings*

- o *Panic attacks*

- o *Obsessive thoughts*

- o *Phobias*

- o *Other*

Check any chronic physical symptoms you have that might be associated with anxiety.

- o *Rapid or irregular heartbeats*

- o *Tension headaches*

- o *Tightening in chest or other chest pain*

- o *Digestive problems*

- o *Sweaty palms*

- o *Other*

Check the activities you have been doing to relieve anxiety.

- o *Talking to friends*

- o *Self-help techniques*

- o *Exercise*

- o *Hobbies*

- *Therapies — list type*

- *Drugs — list any side effects*

- *Addictive behaviors — describe (coffee, smoking, alcohol, shopping, other)*

- *Nutrition — describe (diet, herbs, vitamins, other)*

- *Other*

As you read this book and practice the tools and techniques, periodically review the items you checked to see which have changed and which you still would like to change. Use the tools to gain the insight and motivation you need to make those changes.

chapter 2

What Makes You Anxious?

Don't forget that little emotions are the great captains of our lives.

—Vincent van Gogh

At the root of anxiety is some type of fear. Fear arises when your security or stability is threatened. While fear is designed to warn you of real danger, the few times the danger is real are offset by the thousands of times it isn't. Philosophies, religions, and a myriad of therapies and books talk about overcoming fear. But for all the attention to the subject, fear is still one of the last things that most people are actually able to let go of. Positive thinking and affirmations alone won't do it. You can't visualize, think, rationalize, or affirm your fears away, because feeling and beliefs call the shots. If you don't feel and deeply believe what you're affirming, the fear will keep recurring and even engender other out-of-control reactions like anger, withdrawal, or depression. That's why, even after all the well-intentioned advice and attempts, many still feel helpless about ever really getting rid of their fears.

Transforming anxiety is not about numbing fears or denying real threats. It starts with managing your emotional investment in fear feelings and projections. Jane Phillimore, author of an excellent article on anxiety, gives some typical examples of how emotional investment occurs. "'I worry that I'm making myself ill by worrying. I worry I'm becoming so tired that I soon won't be able to think, that I'll lose control and go crazy. Yet I still can't stop worrying'… For others something as simple as their child or partner being thirty minutes late coming home can trigger anxiety that they have been run over by a bus. Then they add imagination to the projection, making it worse and worse. There is a story about a businessman who said his mind is '…running about like hitting a tennis racket again and again. You start to ask your-self, am I doing it all right, you question your own ability, question yourself as a human being, and when you're like that and it goes on and on, it's vicious'" (Phillimore 2001).

Anxiety Habits

What the examples above illustrate are anxiety habits created by *emotional investment* in the anxiety. Most people don't think of anxiety as a habit. They think it's something happening to them rather than something they are creating. Thinking this isn't bad; it's only human. But nothing will change until people take responsibility for investing in anxiety thoughts and reactions. Taking responsibility isn't judging or blaming yourself, which goes nowhere. Judgment and blame only deflect responsibility and drain your energy. Taking responsibility starts with realizing that you are allowing negative projections to control you.

An anxiety habit often starts by projecting worst-case scenarios of what might happen—in the world; in your workplace, home, or family; and personally — how someone will talk to you, respond, or treat you. You can create storage bins of anxiety projections; then a fear or worry can pop out of storage with the least little trigger, especially when you're tired or worn down. Worry can start with just one feeling or perception followed by a thought, then by a feeling, then another thought, then another feeling — until you are wound in an anxiety loop. You can end up downright distraught or angry about what *might* happen.

We knew an accomplished publisher who was skilled at editing everyone else's stories but couldn't edit her own projections. "I walk to the train station on my way to work," she said, "and have angry conversations in my head rehearsing how I am going to defend myself with people I have upcoming phone appointments with that day. It's crazy, but I always assume the worst. I'm often exhausted by 11:00 A.M."

The mind likes to search for and examine all the angles it can find related to worst-case scenarios. This is a very private, internal process where you drain your energy and then drain it some more. Fear, insecurities, comparisons, and self-image bombers make up most people's anxiety arsenal. Some anxiety habits are so familiar they simply go unnoticed. You can be living for so long with a fear of being rejected, snubbed, left out, a failure, unaccomplished, or unable to communicate that you adapt to it. You can get so used to anxious or apprehensive feelings that it just wouldn't feel natural to be without them. Anxieties that have become ingrained are just there. They rule your life, and you never even noticed you handed over your power to them.

If fear were like a pat of butter, anxiety would be like spreading it with a knife, taking those fearful thoughts and emotions and working them over, day and night, week after week. This kind of anxiety is a self-defeating habit because it isn't based on fact and doesn't resolve anything. Your repetition of it isn't perfecting a useful skill; it's dulling your feeling world while draining your energy. Here's a simple illustration of what an anxiety habit can sound like in your head.

Let's say you were invited on a family camping trip and feel like you have to go, although you really don't want to. Immediately you start to negatively project into the future, triggering anxious feelings. What if it rains? What if you get poison oak? What if your sister-in-law takes over the cooking the whole weekend and makes you miserable? What if someone asks you a question about some touchy issue? Does this sound familiar?

You can probably parallel this illustration with similar situations in your life. Whatever your personal worst-case scenario, you project it and then fear it as if it were a done deal. Projecting fear slams the door on the heart. Clarity and intuition cannot get in. Most fears are by-products of projecting insecurity onto simple, everyday issues that eat you up. The mind projects with thoughts like "Should I do this or say that? What if they don't like me?" "Should I sit next to this person? What if he judges me?" These insecurity projections accumulate into the anxiety habit.

Anxiety habits can lead to nervous system and biochemical imbalances and cause panic attacks or other physical symptoms. More anxiety or even sheer terror can arise from projecting that you may be stuck in a situation where you would go into a panic attack. If you suffer from panic attacks, you may fear you are going crazy or fear what other people will think of you if you lose control. This is a logical progression of an anxiety habit. The hopeful news is that you *can* transform anxiety habits, as many people are doing.

But first it helps to understand the underlying psychological mechanisms.

True Care Versus Overcare

Overcare about people, issues, things, or yourself is the most common cause of anxiety. What often happens is that you get overidentified or overattached to what you care about, whether it's a relationship, a work issue, how you look, or what might happen. Overidentity occurs when your sense of self-worth becomes overly invested in a person or issue. When you get overidentified—whether with your spouse or child, with your job, with money, or with a social issue—your care turns into overcare. You stay worried or anxious, and your energy gets drained. Too much overcare can wear you out until you end up not caring anymore.

> *Don's situation is a good example of overidentity. He was so overidentified with his projects and performance at work that it took a toll on his people skills. Whenever Don's boss would call and leave him a voice mail, he would anxiously redial his boss every two minutes and wouldn't talk to anyone else until he could reach him. Don lost clients and his coworkers felt put off. He was overly concerned with his projects and performance and overattached to what his boss might think, because to him, his work was his identity. Don was unable to see that his overidentity led to a blind perfectionism that eventually cost him his job. Angry after he was fired, Don stopped caring about getting another job. He refused to leave the house and sank into depression.*

One of the first steps in transforming anxiety is to understand the difference between real care and overcare.

When the basic human need to care gets out of balance, people end up overcaring or not caring enough. Most people know what not-enough care feels like but may not be aware of the debilitating effects of overcare.

> *When Bonnie first heard the word "overcare," she knew what it meant immediately. She could see overcare in herself and in her friends clearly. Bonnie had been a passionate advocate for social causes, but was worn out from overcaring. She suffered panic attacks and was on antidepressants like so many other people she knew. She'd finally withdrawn from her friends because they were all going through trying times and it depressed her more to be around them.*

When you are trapped in overcare, like Bonnie, life loses its luster and meaning, just as it does when you stop caring at all. It's through true care that people find value and positive meaning in life. Research shows that genuine feelings of care, such as when people feel warmly connected with others and cared about or when they feel a sense of achievement, pride, or self-esteem, help to increase their long-term psychological well-being (Fredrickson 2000).

Nature's Care Programming

Nature has programmed care right into the DNA. In many species, care is associated with nurturing. Watch a mother lovingly attend her newborn or a father sacrifice his own meal to feed the family, and you'll see that nurturing is a natural response. When you love, you care, and when you care, you take care of, or nurture, others. Care generates a sense of security and connection, a life-affirming bond.

Yet, surprisingly, if you look up "care" in most dictionaries, the first definitions often refer to "a troubled or burdened state of mind; worry; a disquieted state of mixed uncertainty, apprehension, and responsibility; a cause for such anxiety; painstaking or watchful attention." But this is what we are calling overcare. True care shows up several lines later in our Webster's definition: "to feel love for, to look after, provide for, attend to." For many in society, care has become overcare instead—a source of burden, worry, anxiety, and even manipulation, rather than a nurturing experience.

If you're like most anxiety sufferers, your root motive is to care. And that's good. You care that you look good, do a good job, get a promotion, are thought well of, or have enough money to provide for the well-being of your children or help take care of others. But when you don't manage overidentity or overattachment to those cares, they turn into overcare, and often without realizing it, you end up frustrated or anxious, drained and exhausted.

> *Jon and Sandi spent their lives rushing — rushing to fix breakfast; rushing to get the kids to school; rushing themselves to work; rushing the kids to after-school lessons, soccer, swim team, theater; rushing to get dinner; rushing to clean the house and pay the bills; then dropping exhausted into bed only to have to rise early the next day to do it all again. Their schedule was frustrating and anxiety producing to both of them as well as to the kids. They felt bad that they didn't have much family time together but couldn't see any way out. They said they did it because they cared and wanted their children to have the best.*

The Overcare Phenomenon

Care is noble, but overcare—rushing to keep a superhuman schedule because you're afraid of what might happen if you stop or slow down—will drain your energy and vitality in life. In the same way, worrying about others, a common type of overcare, can backfire because it often makes people feel smothered or manipulated, which can cause them to push you away.

> *Celeste believed that she wasn't a loving mother to her children unless she was constantly worrying about them. Even though the children were thirty-five and forty-two, she worried when they had a cold; worried that something might happen when they went on vacation; and when they visited, she worried whether they were dressed warmly enough when they went outdoors, just as she had always done since they were little. After all, she was a mother, and this is what mothers do. To Celeste, her worry (which translates as overcare) expressed her love for them. To the kids, who were now adults, Celeste's overcare made them want to avoid her. As a result, they rarely called or visited.*
>
> *Celeste developed anxiety-related health problems, according to her doctor, but she was unaware (in denial) of the fact that she was feeling anxiety. Celeste equated worrying about her children with love, and she saw it as an endearing quality. What she was unable to see was how her overcare was more about her remaining in the role she had played all her life than it was about true care. The role was familiar and had defined her sense of who she was. She didn't see that everything could improve across the board if she would give herself permission to move into a more balanced type of care with her children.*

You've probably known mothers or fathers like Celeste, who don't feel like they are caring unless they are worrying and anxious about their children. Years ago when Doc Childre, one of the authors of this book, was looking at his own life, he recognized that this was also true for him. "The more I cared for family, friends, work, or issues, the more worry and anxiety I had about them. What I cared most about kept giving me the most stress. 'Why?' I kept asking myself. 'Well, because I care,' I told myself. And I saw that this was true for most people. Suddenly a lightbulb went on inside and many types of stress began to make sense."

Most of the time when people get anxious, they are caring about something, but in a draining and usually ineffective way. Doc saw that most of his own and other people's problems started with care. But then the mind would take that care and turn it into worry and stress. So, Doc coined the term "overcare" to describe the kind of care that creates anxiety and stress. Overload, overwhelm, going overboard, overcare—all these terms mean doing too much to the point of undoing or downfall. Overcare is as old as history and causes endless misery. It affects men as well as women. Overcare occurs when the mind turns your genuinely caring intentions into a mental and emotional drain.

Overcare and Aging

Elissa Epel, a researcher at University of California, San Francisco, studied the cells of mothers of sick children to see if caregiving stress affected part of the chromosome called a telomere. Telomeres are thought to be biological markers of aging. As people get older, telomeres naturally shrink. When the telomere gets too short to work properly, cells all over the body start to sicken or die—and diseases of old age set in.

Caregiving stress is often experienced as worry and anxiety. Epel's study found that the longer women had been caring for a child with a serious illness, the shorter their telomeres, suggesting rapid aging. But alarmingly, the study also found that high stress also affected the telomeres in the stressed-out mothers of healthy kids in the control group. The mothers who felt they were near burnout in either group had shorter telomeres. In fact, when the researchers looked only at stressed-out women in either group, they found a dramatic sign of damaged telomeres. The problem wasn't caring for a sick child; it was the stress of being near burnout. According to Epel, the amount of telomeric DNA these women had last was equivalent to the amount one would expect to lose in ten years of aging (Epel et al. 2004).

Overattachment

Closely related to overcare is overattachment. Your care becomes overattached because you're afraid of losing the thing you care so much about. Or you overly attach yourself to someone, some place, some issue, or some thing in order to receive confirmation that you are valued. Overattachment can lead to a continuous running anxiety as you try to maintain that positive feedback. Overattachment sucks energy from others and makes you a victim of whether or not they approve of you. It can make you overcontrolling and repress those you love while it suffocates your inner peace and security.

> *Joan and Brad had been married for four years. Brad felt he couldn't do anything without being under the ever-present watchful eye of Joan. As for Joan, she just wanted him to know she was there for him. When they went to parties, Joan would spend the whole evening trying to make sure that Brad was having a good time. She would constantly ask him if he wanted another drink or let him know who*

was coming into the room in case he wanted to talk with them. Brad felt so suffocated by Joan's overattachment that he insisted on going to a marriage counselor.

Because Joan felt so insecure about her own value and identity, she felt the need to create a reason (over-attachment) for Brad to keep her around and not "stray." Brad was feeling stifled and choked by the obsessive atten-tion. Brad and Joan eventually divorced, leaving Joan feel-ing rejected and betrayed, and not understanding why.

The draining cycle begins as you overidentify with a position, a situation, an issue, or a person you care about—in other words, you identify too much. You begin to overcare and want things to go a certain way. You get overattached to how you want things to turn out and are unable to see other options. You're less able to let go of that issue, that situation, or that person. When you overattach, you become obsessive. And, ironically, just the opposite of what you want usually happens as a result—you get fired instead of promoted, or a person you want to bring closer avoids you. And you are astonished. After all, you cared so much!

This self-destructive cycle is insidious. Overcare and overattachment can quickly spread to others and infect an entire family or workplace like an emotional virus. Here's an example of how the emotional virus typically spreads. See if you can find similar examples in your life.

The Emotional Virus

Risa, a coworker, storms into your office anxious and upset because of what Joe, a manager, said about a project that Risa's been working on. "Can you believe that?" she hisses. "No way!" you exclaim. You feel your anger ris-ing. You're identifying. Risa goes on, laying out what she heard in the lunchroom. As she's talking, your mind is going a mile a minute, recalling similar incidents that have happened to you. Your anger grows stronger. Now both of you are judging and blaming Joe. You are totally overidentified. Blood pressure rising, you start worrying about what will happen. Will that bozo tell the boss? Will Risa get stonewalled? What will you do? Will you be asked to take sides? Anxiety creeps in. You're now in overcare. You'd better protect your turf. You're already creating your strategy: Hold onto the report you're working on and don't let him see it. Your mind is manipulating next steps. Who else should you tell? Your anxiety has turned to fear. You're overattached to this whole situation. The next day you find out that Joe never said that. It was a rumor Risa heard from someone else at lunch.

This kind of thing happens every day for many of us, and it's energy spent and wasted. Even if Joe *had* said that, if you overidentify, you become the victim—the victim of your own and others' emotional chaos.

When you look at the world through the eyes of over-identity, overattachment, and overcare, you quickly take sides based on partial information. This is what's fueling the growing epidemics of stress, anxiety, and depression. The result is often a blind refusal to understand another's point of view. This is what's behind many divorces, conflicts, riots, and wars.

If you want to help those you care about or even the world, you need to start with yourself. When you don't manage overcare or overattachment, they become a habit. Your emotional stamina is drained, and that leads to a lackluster quality in day-to-day experiences. When emotional quality is low, you mechanically operate at half-mast; your peace, fun, and power to adapt are significantly reduced. You stay so stressed or anxious that you end up feeling ineffective, or that you've cared too much and can't care anymore.

Energized emotional involvement and passion toward a goal are different from worry. They open the mind to creative possibilities. But anxiety closes the mind and can delay accomplishment of a goal or spoil its celebration.

Overcare in one area often results in a lack of care in another area. It's like squeezing a balloon at one end so that it bulges at the other end. This lack of balance in care can result in small annoyances ruining people's joy in life. A television producer shared a quote attributed to Winston Churchill, saying, "It's the broken shoelaces that destroy men's lives." She added that she finds these words coming to mind often. "I can control my anger and my bigger emotions. It's not the big things that get to me anymore; the little things are what get me all day long and worry me." A friend describes it this way: "Stress is death from a thousand paper cuts. You never know how many you can handle before it's too much."

Expectation and Perfectionism

Another form of overcare is unreasonable expectations of others or yourself. Most people place the heaviest expectations on themselves. You expect yourself to live up to an image or ideal, then you overcare and feel guilty when you don't measure up. Here's an example: Andy, a friend of ours, valiantly set out to take care of his health. He planned a low-fat diet and bought an expensive rowing machine. Five days later, he still hadn't used the machine and had blown his diet with a chocolate mousse he couldn't refuse.

Andy had unrealistic expectations of himself and guilt from not achieving his expectations. Perfectionism generates inflexible attitudes and all-or-nothing thinking, which is what plagues Andy. He expects perfection in whatever he does. He goes all out in his planning, whether for weight loss or finding the right woman to date or the right house to buy, and often ends up disappointed. Perfectionism is a rigidity that insists that things have to be a certain way, and if they are not, then something is wrong and anxiety results. When you assess life from a perfectionist viewpoint, you tend to *overpersonalize* things that don't go your way. You feel not good enough or better than others, and this can lead you into performance anxiety, self-pity, or blame. Yet it's you who is setting idealistic or unrealistic expectations from overcare.

Identifying Overcare

Realize there is often a very fine line between true care, which is renewing and effective, and overcare, which is draining. You can learn to distinguish between them by how they make you feel. To start with, ask yourself, "Is what I care about stress producing or stress reducing?" If it's stress producing, you know there's overcare involved and it's draining your energy. If it's stress reducing, that's where your care is in balance, regenerative and adding to your energy.

Now think back to a time when you cared about something, and cared so much that you found yourself anxious. Next, think back to a time when you cared about something and it felt great. That's the difference you're looking for in your feeling world. If you recognize the feelings or emotions that follow your attempts to care, you'll start to understand when your care is stress producing, rather than being a renewing experience.

A nurse at one of our seminars talked about "compassion fatigue," a term that has become popular at the hospital where she works. During the seminar she realized that when she feels compassion it renews her. The fatigue and drain came when her compassion turned into feelings of stress from overcare and overidentity. It's important to learn the language of your feeling world.

✎ *Make a list in your mind or on paper of who and what you care about most to see where you are draining or adding to your energy. Create a "Releasing Overcare and Overidentity Worksheet – A Picture of My Care" in your journal, following the instructions below. This exercise will help you get a picture of your care and identify overcares, overidentities, and overattachments that create anxiety. In the next few chapters, you'll learn how to cut through them.*

Create three vertical columns across a piece of paper. Label the first column "What I Care About" and under the heading list the people, issues, and things you care most about in your life. Label the second column "Scale 0–5," then assign a number (with 0 being the lowest and 5 being the most extreme) to how much overcare you have around this person, item, or issue. Head the third column "Overcare Thoughts, Feelings, Actions" and describe how you think, feel, and act about what you are overcaring about. Below there are two examples.

What I Care About	Scale (0–5)	Overcare Thoughts, Feelings, Actions
My elderly father	*5*	*Whatever I do for him never seems good enough; I get frustrated, anxious, yell at him, and feel bad.*
My health/ appearance	*4*	*I worry about my health and aging. I diet and exercise, then eat the wrong foods and get too busy to exercise. I feel guilty all the time.*

Remember as you do this exercise that overcare is only human. It's not bad. It's just that when taken to extremes, it generates anxiety and guilt. Anxiety isn't bad either. It's just not a very fun or effective way to live. Overcare and anxiety rarely give you intelligent solutions. They can't. They block the brain's ability to see solutions, and that's why the mind keeps looping around, unable to find a way out.

See where expectation, perfectionism, or performance anxiety are involved in the overcares you listed above. As you look at your life through the lens of overcare, you can see how a lot of your anxiety and low energy is based on real care that slipped into overcare. In fact, "A Picture of My Care" might be better named "A Picture of My Anxiety." Recognizing this can be a relief in itself. After all, *you do care.*

Releasing Overcare

The HeartMath tools, techniques, and examples in this book will show you how to release overcare and bring it back to true care. The tools are designed to help you transform overcare and anxiety—mentally, emotionally, and physically. It takes practice to repattern an anxiety habit, but you can start seeing results immediately. You may find that relinquishing overcare in even one area will release overcare and anxiety about other areas at the same time. Make notes on your insights as you practice the tools and techniques in the following chapters.

Heart Intelligence— The Essence of Hope

So many people believe that life has to be anxiety-ridden and painful, and that where there is no pain there is no gain. Religions have taught that the soul matures through trial by fire

— self-doubt, angst, heartache, and despair. Through learning to connect with your heart intelligence, you realize that you don't have to keep learning that way. <u>Heart intelligence is the harmonization of feelings and thoughts, giving you balance and intuitive common sense</u>. You have compassion for your struggles and those of others but see how to rise up to new heights of emotional freedom. It's heart intelligence that *empowers* you to transform anxiety, guilt, anger, and stress and move on from there. With heart intelligence, you invite in more of your spirit and you see life through new eyes. You build true care that feels good and renews you. You live life with depth and passion—and your downtime and recovery happen a lot faster. You unravel the mysteries of life with far less effort and time wasted.

Cutting through overcare is like separating the wheat of your true care from the chaff of your anxiety and insecurities. The result is that life has enhanced value and positive meaning for you. You bring forth potentials hidden within your heart that you didn't know were there. You become more of who you really are. Experiencing this brings a tremendous sense of hope. And with hope comes renewed energy and passion for life.

chapter 3

Transforming Overcare and Anxiety Triggers

*When man is serene, the pulse of the heart flows
and connects, just as pearls are joined together or
like a string of red jade, then one can talk about a
healthy heart.*

— *The Yellow Emperor's Canon
of Internal Medicine,* 2500 B.C.

You won't stop all overcare and anxiety triggers. They're
standard human reactions. But you can stop the behaviors
they generate that drain your energy and spirit. Doc Childre,
along with researchers at the Institute of HeartMath, has
developed powerful yet simple tools and techniques that
quickly improve how you feel, think, and perceive. With just
a little practice, you will start to transform overcare and anxiety reactions into balanced care and more ease. These tools
can seem too simple, but it's their simplicity that makes them
work. They harness the power of your heart to give you the
intelligence and power you need to make the changes you
want. Here's how they work.

The Role of the Heart in Transforming Anxiety

The physical heart sets the rhythm and pace for the whole body. The respiratory and digestive systems and brain waves also generate rhythms, although they are not as strong as the heart's rhythm. Most people don't realize that the heartbeat produces forty to sixty times more electrical amplitude than the brain and broadcasts an electrical signal that permeates every cell in the body. The strength of the heart's magnetic field is *five thousand times greater* than the field generated by the brain, and it can be measured several feet away from the body in all directions (McCraty 2004).

The Heart-Brain

Your heart also has its own nervous system, or "brain in the heart," containing around forty thousand neurons. This heart-brain can sense, feel, learn, remember, and process information (Armour 2003; Armour and Kember 2004). There are more nerves going from your heart up to your brain than from your brain to your heart (Cameron 2002). This has profound implications. The rhythmic beating pattern of your heart tells the brain how the body feels. With every beat, your heart sends neural messages to the parts of your brain that govern emotion and higher reasoning capacities (Sandman, Walker, and Berka 1982; Frysinger and Harper 1990; McCraty, Atkinson, and Bradley 2004). Any change in the rhythmic pattern of your heart alters the pattern of neural activity that your brain receives, and affects the way you feel and how your brain processes information (McCraty et al. 2005).

Synchronizing Your Rhythms

When your heart's rhythms are harmonious, they create a coherent waveform that helps bring other internal systems into synchronization, entrainment, and alignment. We will be using these scientific terms throughout the book. In physics, when the rhythms of two or more systems synchronize and lock in to the same frequency, it's called *entrainment*. Systems that entrain to each other operate with increased harmony, efficiency, and flow. You can see examples of entrainment when several pendulum clocks all entrain to the beat of the clock with the strongest pendulum, or when a flock of birds or a school of fish moves together in synchronized harmony.

Scientific studies show that positive emotions long associated with the heart, like love, care, compassion, and appreciation, quickly bring heart rhythms into a coherent waveform, as shown in figure 1 (McCraty et al. 1995; Tiller, McCraty, and Atkinson 1996). Coherent heart rhythms pull your brain waves into more synchronization with the heart, which helps bring alignment to your mind and emotions. When mind and emotions align with the heart, mental clarity and intuitive perception improve. Studies have found that when participants' heart rhythms were coherent, their cognitive performance significantly improved (McCraty et al. 2005). A further study also found a significant change in frontal lobe activity that was related to increased heart rhythm coherence and the heart's input to the brain (McCraty, Atkinson, and Bradley 2004). Coherent heart rhythm patterns evoke feelings of security and well-being.

When you're worried, frustrated, or anxious, your heart's rhythmic pattern becomes irregular and chaotic looking, creating an incoherent waveform like the one in figure 2. When this occurs, the different branches of your nervous system are pushing and pulling against each other, and your brain and heart get out of sync. This creates stress: You can't think as clearly, and your memory can jam due to internal "static" or "noise" in your system. Worry, anxiety, and frustration are stress generators.

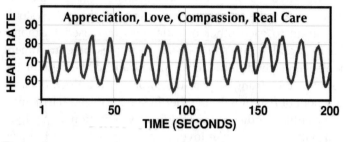

Figure 1

Figure 1 shows the heart rhythm pattern typical of appreciation and other positive feelings. This smooth heart rhythm, measured by heart rate variability (HRV), is what scientists call a highly ordered or *coherent* pattern, and is a sign of good health and emotional balance.

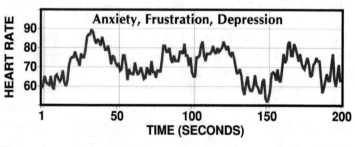

Figure 2

Figure 2 shows the irregular, jerky heart rhythm pattern typical of stressful feelings, which include anxiety, frustration, anger, or depression. This jerky pattern is what scientists call an *incoherent* pattern.

So what can send your heart rhythms into incoherent patterns? Whenever you move or engage in activity, your heart rhythm naturally shifts and then settles back to its baseline pattern. An incoherent baseline pattern results from many factors, but one of the strongest influences is ongoing negative thoughts and negative feelings (McCraty et al. 1995; Tiller, McCraty, and Atkinson 1996).

The Negativity Bias

Despite people's best intentions, a "negativity bias" — a natural tendency to focus on thoughts and emotions perceived as negative — is built into humans as a survival mechanism. Although most people say that they love, care, and appreciate, if they really stop to notice their inner states, they may be shocked to find that they are assuming these qualities more than they are actually feeling them. Instead, what they feel and dwell on more of the time are negative emotions like worry, frustration, fear, and insecurity. As negative feelings are rehashed, they become so familiar they form baseline patterns that shape identity. For example, children of anxious parents tend to also become anxious (Beidel and Turner 1997). The body defaults to what's familiar even when it's dysfunctional. This serves to perpetuate the cycle of anxiety and anxiety disorders.

Through learning to use Tools in Action to bring your physiology into more coherence and synchronization, you can transform negative emotions and bring more intuitive perception into your awareness. As you practice methods to create coherence, more enjoyable states will progressively replace dysfunctional patterns as your familiar way of being. You will improve your baseline heart rhythm pattern, which also improves your health and vitality and slows premature aging.

Emotion Admittance

You can't transform negative emotions until you learn to admit what you are feeling and how your body is responding. By admitting a feeling, whatever it is—worry, anxiety, frustration, anger, hurt, resistance, numbness, or even a vague disturbance you can't put your finger on—you slow down the emotional energy running through your system. Being honest about naming what you are feeling helps regulate your emotional energy and gives you more power. Here's an example of what happens when people don't admit and regulate the energy in their emotions.

> *John calls his wife from work and has an anxious reaction to something she says. He goes to a meeting with his project team, but the disturbed feeling lingers. John can't focus and can hardly hear what is being said. He keeps up with the meeting agenda, yet, inside, his thoughts keep surging back over the things that bothered him about the call. He keeps trying to fight them and quell the disturbance so he can be present for the meeting, but anxious feelings keep disturbing his internal world. Soon he feels dull and drained inside. That one conversation creates an emotional churning that John drags around the rest of the day. When he gets home that night, his wife seems happy to see him, as if nothing had happened. Not wanting to cause an argument, John plops down in front of the TV to try to forget the whole thing. He goes to bed exhausted, still bothered inside.*

John's day could have gone completely differently if he had taken a moment to stop and admit what he was feeling. By admitting and naming what you're feeling, you begin regulating the emotional energy. You then can redirect emotional energy to work for you instead of draining your entire day.

Feelings are like a code that contains information. You have to name and admit feelings to decipher the code and allow intuitive perceptions to come to you. Most people who suffer from anxiety have difficulty admitting feelings. The feelings back up in your system, causing more anxiety. As the turbulence of anxiety churns in the subconscious and plays out in your thoughts and actions, it's called *emotional processing*. You can try to suppress it, but the processing still runs in the background of your thoughts and feelings and the drain of energy goes on and on. This festering "understuff" can cause fatigue, sleep disorders, hormone imbalances, health problems, and premature aging. You can go into a state of resignation that things won't change, and your self-worth suffers.

The idea of admitting your emotions can make you feel vulnerable. You may worry that you'll be engulfed by them. But the opposite happens. As soon as you honestly admit you're feeling anxious, you start to diminish its power over you. But then you don't stop there. As you use one of the tools you'll learn here, you can neutralize the understuff and start to ease out the disturbing feeling or attitude. Even a little ease can bring a more balance perspective.

Notice and Ease is a basic tool in action for admitting emotions. Greg describes his experience practicing Notice and Ease:

> *I was aware of a stream of thoughts most of the time, but I didn't realize there's a stream of emotions going on all the time as well. I really don't think most*

*people realize this either. Practicing being more aware
of how I feel about issues has made me aware of a
stream of understuff, and telling myself to "Notice
and Ease" is giving me choice over it.*

You can learn to release anxiety or other stressful feelings and stop their energy drain by doing the following simple steps.

Look at the list of disturbed feelings below. Note which ones
you experience frequently.

o *tense*	o *resentful*	o *fearful*
o *worried*	o *guilty*	o *blaming*
o *edgy*	o *blocked*	o *numb*
o *anxious*	o *bored*	o *stubborn*
o *overwhelmed*	o *sad*	o *resistant*
o *angst-ridden*	o *self-blaming*	
o *angry*	o *depressed*	

Tool: Notice and Ease

Step 1. Notice and admit what you are feeling.

Step 2. Try to name the feeling.

Step 3. Tell yourself to e-a-s-e — as you gently focus in your
heart, relax as you breathe, and e-a-s-e the stress out.

Practice becoming more conscious of these feelings as they come up. Don't be afraid to admit them. Practice Notice and Ease and you will start to gain power over them. Try an experiment for a day. Each time one of these disturbed feelings arises, go through the steps of the Notice and Ease tool. At the end of the day, note which disturbed feelings were most frequent and what happened as you eased them out.

Emotion Refocusing

The next HeartMath tool to learn is a simple yet powerful tool for emotion refocusing. It's called the Power of Neutral. It teaches you to use the rhythmic power of your heart to bring your mind, emotions, and physiology to a state of neutral that can lessen or stop many anxiety triggers. Think of neutral as a "time-out zone" where you can step back, neutralize your emotions, and see more options with clarity. It will help clear your mental screen and prevent static buildup from understuff and the anxiety it creates.

Tool: Power of Neutral

Step 1. Take a time-out, breathing slowly and deeply. Imagine the air entering and leaving through the heart area or the center of your chest.

Step 2. Try to disengage from your stressful thoughts and worried feelings as you continue to breathe.

Step 3. Continue the process until you have neutralized the emotional charge.

You use step 1 as soon as you feel your emotions start-ing to amp up. First you want to take a time-out by choosing to step back from your emotions. Heart breathing in step 1 helps draw the energy out of your head, where negative thoughts and feelings get amplified. Breathe slowly and deeply in a casual way. Imagine the air entering and leaving through the center of your chest and heart area.

In step 2, disengage from your stressful thoughts and feelings as you continue to breathe. Just having the intent to disengage can help you release a lot of the emotional energy.

In step 3, you continue the process until you have chilled out and neutralized the emotional charge. This doesn't mean your worry, anxiety, or other stressful feeling will have totally evaporated. It just means that the charged energy has been taken out and you have stopped the stress accumula-tion. Even if you can't totally neutralize anxiety in the moment, just the effort to shift into neutral will stop the accu-mulation of anxiety. You now have a chance to regroup your energies and refocus. One of the things that helps to get to neutral is asking yourself, "Do I really want to keep draining energy and stressing about the situation?"

For example, right before a situation that normally makes you anxious, you start projecting that you will panic or be judged by others. This is the perfect time to use Power of Neutral—otherwise your emotional reaction will take over and drain you through the situation. You build your power to tell intrusive disturbing thoughts and feelings, "Thanks for stopping by, but I'm not going to feed you," and mean it.

Performance Anxiety

Learn to practice Power of Neutral when you have per-formance anxiety, like when you are afraid to express your

thoughts or feelings for fear someone will judge you. By chill-
ing out before jumping to conclusions, your wise self can talk
things through with your confused and worried self and save
you a lot of problems. That wise self is your heart intelligence. Learn to practice Power of Neutral any time you need
a feeling of neutral for more objective clarity. You will gain
mental flexibility and free energy.

It's usually cumulative overcares and anxieties along
with the inability to express your feelings that cause undercurrents of anxiety. The accumulation can build up over time
and feel like an inner resistance or heaviness when you try to
go to neutral. It's nothing to worry about. Let go of any performance anxiety about whether you're doing it right. Just
hold the attitude and intent of neutral and it will start to dis-
lodge some of the accumulation.

If the anxiety won't let up, try to disengage from the situation and immerse yourself in something you're interested
in to distract yourself. Often, telling yourself "It's no big
deal" or taking the significance out and moving on to something else is your best approach. As you practice emotion
admittance with Notice and Ease and emotion refocusing
with the Power of Neutral, the strength of the anxiety and
feelings of resistance will start to dissolve.

*Take a look at the Releasing Overcare and Overidentity
worksheet you created in chapter 2. Are there any overcare
issues that keep adding static buildup and just don't seem to
go away? Pick one and practice the Power of Neutral tool. Go
through the steps and see if you can take out some of the
significance or emotional investment you've assigned to it.
Don't worry if you can't get totally neutral. Just experiencing
a little less charge is a great start. Try the Power of Neutral
tool on a few more overcare issues. See if you can find a feeling*

of neutral that brings more objective clarity or more ease.
Practice Power of Neutral several times a day, whether or not
an overcare trigger comes up, to learn the tool and get in the
habit of using it. It will then be easier to remember to use
Power of Neutral when you need it.

Practicing Neutral in Communications

Communication problems are a major cause of anxiety.
You may feel you're not being heard or you feel misunderstood, wrongly blamed, or unfairly treated. Other common
anxiety-producing communication problems are feeling hurt
by what someone says, being unable to say what you really
mean or feel, or feeling pressured into decisions you are confused about or don't agree with. You can use the Power of
Neutral tool to improve communication. You will find that as
you use Power of Neutral *before you speak*, then speak genuinely from your heart, you are likely to express yourself more
clearly and the other person is more likely to hear you at a
deeper level.

Especially use the Power of Neutral tool while listening
to yourself or others. The mind listens to words, while the
heart can perceive feelings and the real meaning behind
words. Practice letting interactions with yourself and others
be guided from the heart. As you use Power of Neutral, ask
yourself, "What is my heart feeling about the situation?"
Then ask yourself, "What would be a more effective attitude?" It's not bad to have negative thoughts or feelings. Just
take responsibility to clean up the energies with Power of
Neutral.

Ginger explains how practicing Power of Neutral helped
her: "I used to find myself feeling misunderstood all the
time. I'd try to be neutral, but could hear myself saying

*to others, 'Well, all I meant was . . .' I was so convinced
that I knew what others were thinking of me that I was
constantly defending myself and my ideas." Ginger found
that by using the Power of Neutral tool things changed.
After going through the steps, she'd tell herself, "Hold to
neutral." She would stay centered in her heart, and if she
felt herself getting anxious, she'd ask herself, "What if
it's not like I'm thinking it is?" Asking that question
began to yield results. "I began to see waves of assump-
tions come up in my mind that I never realized were
behind a lot of my thoughts," she says. "But I really had
to stay in my heart and hold onto neutral to see this."*

The neutral place Ginger found is actually a place of
freedom — freedom to see your own reactions — and freedom
to choose not to buy into them. Neutral is a place where you
gain empowerment to have real choice.

Emotion Restructuring

Positive emotions have been shown to improve health and
increase longevity (Blakeslee 1997; Danner, Snowdon, and
Friesen 2001), while promoting helpfulness, generosity, and
effective cooperation (Isen 1987). Researchers in a field called
positive psychology are finding that positive emotions are far
more important to mental health and physical well-being
than scientists had ever realized (Snyder and Lopez 2002).
University of Michigan researcher Barbara Fredrickson says,
"Positive emotions can have effects beyond making people
'feel good' or improving their subjective experiences of life.
They also have the potential to broaden people's habitual
modes of thinking and build their physical, intellectual, and
social resources" (Fredrickson 2000).

Negative emotions aren't wrong. They are signals that something needs attention. The most effective attention is to take them to neutral and find something to feel positive about so that you can gain new perspectives about the issue. According to researchers, when you're experiencing a negative emotion, the thoughts available to your mind are limited, yielding fixated and more predictable thinking and action. When you're experiencing a positive emotion, more possibilities come into your view. Positive emotions produce patterns of thought that are notably unusual, flexible and inclusive, creative, and receptive, and lead to more creative action (Isen 1998, 1999; Fredrickson 2002).

Positive emotions also have an "undoing effect" on negative emotions. They loosen the hold that negative emotions gain on your brain and body. Positive and negative emotions are fundamentally incompatible because it's hard to experience both simultaneously. This incompatibility accounts for why positive emotions seem to serve as effective antidotes for the lingering effects of negative emotions (Fredrickson 2002).

Cultivating more positive emotional experiences and attitudes results in emotion restructuring—creating new neural pathways in the brain. Fredrickson concludes, "Through experiences of positive emotions people transform themselves, becoming more creative, knowledgeable, resilient, socially integrated, and healthy individuals" (Fredrickson 2002).

Attitude directs how you manage your energy. Negative attitudes generate emotional undercurrents or background noise that can become ingrained and automatic. These undercurrents affect your mood swings, the way you feel overall, and your relationships. By learning to shift to positive attitudes, you increase your emotional stability and resilience.

The Attitude Breathing tool is designed to help you shift out of a negative emotional state into a positive one (psychologically and physiologically). You learn to clear and replace negative attitudes right in the midst of stress or anxiety to gain a more intelligent perspective.

Tool: Attitude Breathing

Step 1. Recognize an unwanted attitude: a feeling or attitude that you want to change. This could be overcare, anxiety, self-judgment, guilt, anger, anything.

Step 2. Identify and breathe a replacement attitude: Select a positive attitude, then breathe the feeling of that new attitude slowly and casually through your heart area. Do this for a while to anchor the new feeling.

Often the appropriate replacement attitude to breathe can be obvious, like balance, nonjudgment, or appreciation. You can use the attitude replacement list below or be open to a new replacement attitude from your intuition. It takes breathing the *feeling* of the new attitude to make it real. For example, if you are worried, you may want to breathe calm, but this requires breathing the feeling a while until you actually feel calmed. Then you have made what we call the *energetic shift*. This means that the turbulent emotional energy in your subconscious has shifted.

Unwanted Feelings and Attitudes	Replacement Feelings and Attitudes
Stressed	Breathe neutral to chill out and revitalize
Anxious	Breathe calm
Overwhelmed	Breathe ease and peace
Fogged/Confused	Breathe neutral for clarity
Angry/Upset	Breathe neutral to cool down
Judgmental	Breathe tolerance or compassion

As you breathe these replacement attitudes, tell yourself to take the "big deal" out, or to take the significance out. Continue the Attitude Breathing until you feel a shift or a change. Remember that even when a negative attitude feels justified, the buildup of negative emotional energy still drains your system. Have a genuine "I mean business" attitude to really move those emotions into a more coherent state and shift your physiology. It could take a few minutes, but it's worth the genuine practice.

See which replacement attitude(s) give you the most relief and write them down. As you practice, you'll discover that each of these replacement attitudes has a different feeling or texture that accompanies it. Feelings also create different hormonal responses. Practiced sincerely, these positive attitudes and emotions all have the power to bring your heart rhythms into more coherence and your mental, emotional, and hormonal systems into synchronization and alignment.

When You Feel Resistance

Some attitudes and anxiety feelings are stubborn and keep recurring. Just keep breathing the new attitude. Remember to breathe slowly and casually and stay focused on the replacement attitude even when you feel resistance. Imagine pulling in and anchoring the new feeling in the heart. You will build new neural pathways and will feel better as you keep it up.

Some people have a difficult time feeling positive attitudes like appreciation, and this can cause anxiety. Peter Gruenewald, MD, general practitioner and medical advisor in the National Health Service and private practice (Bristol and London, United Kingdom), has this advice:

> *I have a patient who suffered with states of anxiety and depression on and off for two years. I advised her to practice the Power of Neutral and Attitude Breathing during the day. When trying to find a feeling of appreciation, she developed strong feelings of anxiety. I advised her to instead breathe calm and select a memory associated with the feeling of inner calm whilst sustaining heart focus. She managed this without any anxiety and felt relaxed and well afterwards. I then advised her to feel appreciation for the new calm she had and start transforming the inner calm into appreciation. This is an effective way to help people feel appreciation.*

✐ *Other Times to Use Attitude Breathing*

To clear hurt and anger. You can use Attitude Breathing to help clear the hurt and anger from old situations you can't change. Just keep breathing a replacement attitude to hurt or anger. Another benefit: Changing your attitude often makes it easier for others to have an attitude shift.

When feeling overwhelmed. Use Attitude Breathing when you are feeling overwhelmed. Breathe e-a-s-e and peace for a minute or so and tell yourself to go a step at a time. You'll draw new creative ways to respond or prioritize that often get overlooked when you're overwhelmed and your senses are jammed.

Before sleep. Focusing on positive replacement attitudes and practicing the Attitude Breathing tool before falling asleep often leads to more peaceful and rejuvenating sleep and reduces carryover of negative thoughts and emotions into the following day. Breathe balance, appreciation, or any replacement attitude for a few minutes after you close your eyes or until you fall asleep.

When you are projecting. Negative projections about what might happen today or tomorrow can surface anytime, but most people are more vulnerable to them in the early morning when they first wake up, or later in the afternoon when they haven't taken a break or are tired. People project their insecurities into the future, which tends to bring up more insecurity. The resulting energy drain is like paying a projection tax. When you tally the accumulated tax from all your projections by the end of an hour or a day, you can see why you may feel a bit down or don't feel as good as you should, even if it was a pretty good day overall. You spent energy and time emotionally reacting to problems you thought you were going to encounter—having to talk to someone you don't like, another hard day like yesterday, too much work ahead of you and never enough time, and so on.

To prevent projecting into the future, as soon as you notice a projection taking hold, stop and use Attitude Breathing for a few moments. Choose a replacement attitude, or breathe an attitude of appreciation to prepare yourself for whatever might happen next. It could be better than you think. Doing this for thirty seconds or longer will build your energy reserves and serve as a reference place to come back to if the projection starts up again. When you see yourself starting to squander your energy in a projection, ask your heart intelligence for guidance and tell yourself, "No, don't go there. I can't afford it. It'll be too much tax, and I've already paid that one before."

> *Janice talks about how she got over her habit of projecting anxieties into the future. "I used to get ready for work in the morning in a totally preoccupied state, running a steady stream of thoughts about what was going to happen that day." After tiring — literally — of the process, Janice decided to try Attitude Breathing. "Now, as soon as I get up and start moving around the room, while my husband sleeps, this is my time to love and appreciate life. I tell myself, 'Breathe love and appreciation' and negative thoughts and feelings aren't allowed. Only love and appreciation." Janice admits, "Of course, it's not perfect; other thoughts and feelings do come up. But I stop them as soon as I can and don't give them any more energy. I just take them right back to the heart and breathe." The results have been subtle yet unmistakable. "It's not like I get into a great burst of love every morning. Most of the time, it's just a soft, gentle feeling — but a good one. This is a special time in which I get in touch with myself and muster up some of the best inside me before I start my day."*

When you are obsessing or worrying. Many people have day-to-day anxiety about decision making, which can lead to obsessive worrying and procrastination.

Linda has this type of anxiety daily: "I worry about what I should make for dinner, worry about how I should write or say things, and worry about most any decision, fearing that I won't pick or do the best option. This contributes to a background worry that things won't work out. I used Notice and Ease, Power of Neutral, and Attitude Breathing. They worked in the moment, but then the worrying would come back. Doc suggested that I try Attitude Breathing in through the heart and then out through the stomach and down through the feet to really anchor my intention and begin to take out the underlying pattern of worry. I find doing that helps ease out the jittery energy and tightness in my emotions. When I find myself spinning around in my mind and overthinking things, breathing out through my feet also helps release me from the hold of my mind. I use it throughout the day even when I'm walking around doing my job."

Tools in Action

The HeartMath tools you have learned in this chapter, Notice and Ease for emotion admittance, Power of Neutral for emotion refocusing, and Attitude Breathing for emotion restructuring, can be used by themselves or together in less than three minutes once you've learned them. We call these Tools in Action, because they help you shift out of anxiety and other draining emotions and attitudes while you're on the go. But you have to actually *use* the tools, not just think about them, for them to work. You will increase your coherence and build new habits and baseline patterns as you practice. You will also find yourself becoming a more balanced, calmer, and wiser person. Power of Neutral and Attitude Breathing especially help you build confidence and self-security. You can use them when you find yourself struggling between what your mind wants and what your heart knows is right. They can help you act on your heart's truth and integrity and make more appropriate decisions. You find security in your own heart as you access and follow the wisdom of your heart intelligence.

Heart Intelligence and Power

Without heart intelligence, the untamed mind and emotions will keep you duped into believing that your vitality is being squandered by circumstances beyond your control. These Tools in Action help you shift to a state of increased psychophysiological coherence, which can bring your entire system—heart, brain, mind, emotions, and nervous system—into a dynamic state of internal flow. In this state, intuitive heart intelligence becomes more available to you. Heart intelligence will help you to adapt to life's challenges and save loads of time and energy that could be lost to fears, anxieties, emotional processing, mental confusion, and poor decisions. Heart intelligence opens pathways from the heart to the brain that give you the information and power you need to be in in control and to free yourself from anxiety.

In the next chapter, you will learn the Cut-Thru technique for clearing anxiety accumulation and the past emotional histories that created it.

chapter 4

Transforming and Clearing Accumulated Anxieties

If each of us sweeps in front of our own steps, the whole world would be clean.

—Goethe

It takes alignment between heart, brain, mind, emotions, and nervous system to release accumulated anxieties. We call this *heart alignment.* By using the power of heart rhythm coherence to create heart alignment, you can cut through accumulated anxieties and free your energy to enjoy your life now.

According to ancient Greek texts, Gordius, king of Phrygia, tied a knot so entwined that no one could untie it. A prophecy foretold that anyone who succeeded in untying the knot would become ruler of all of Asia. Alexander the Great was struggling to figure out the intricacies of how the knot was formed, when in a flash of insight, he realized, "It makes no difference how it's tied!" and cut through the knot with his sword. Alexander the Great went on to become the ruler of Asia.

The expression "cut through" means "get to the heart of the matter." When dealing with anxiety, you don't have time to go through all the details of your past to get relief. You need to cut through. That's why Doc designed the Cut-Thru technique, and shortened the spelling to cut-thru.

The Cut-Thru technique shows you how to cut-thru the Gordian knot of accumulated overcares, anxieties, and fears to become ruler of your own self. Accumulated anxieties are composed of perceptions, feelings, and energy stored in cellular memories. It takes practice to build your coherence power with Cut-Thru, but as you practice, you transform cellular patterns into insight and effective action. You clear anxiety accumulation as you release emotional investment built up around past issues.

Learning to Cut-Thru

Cut-Thru's six short steps were designed to help take you through the process of release. Each time you repeat them with the right attitude, old perceptions, thoughts, and feelings are released from your cells. Approaching the technique with a sincere "I mean business" attitude accelerates the clearing. After you go through the steps a few times, it will get simpler. Eventually the flow of the steps becomes automatic inside and you can just use the quick steps for release.

It's important to read through the explanations of the steps to understand how the process unfolds. The wording of each step is designed to build the coherence you need to release deep issues.

To get started, pick an anxiety issue. Don't pick your most loaded or most stressful issue to start. Pick a minor issue to learn on. Create a Cut-Thru worksheet on a piece of paper or in your journal or notebook (instructions for making the worksheet can be found later in this chapter). Read each step, the explanation, and the example of how Tracy, a customer service manager, used the step. Then practice the step on your issue, and write your response on the Cut-Thru worksheet. Continue with the next steps and do the same. When you finish, look back and read your responses to each step to gain more understanding. Note what your heart is telling you, then take action on your intuition. If you are uncertain, do the steps again to get more clarity.

The Cut-Thru Technique

Step 1. Be aware of how you feel about the issue at hand.

Step 2. Center yourself by breathing in through the heart and out through the solar plexus. Breathe love and appreciation through this area for thirty seconds or longer to help anchor your attention there.

Step 3. Assume objectivity about the feeling or issue — as if it were someone else's problem.

Step 4. Rest in neutral — in your rational, mature heart.

Step 5. Soak and relax any disturbed or perplexing feelings in the compassion of the heart. Dissolve the significance a little at a time. Remember, it's not the problem that causes energy drain as much as the stored significance you have assigned to the problem.

Step 6. After dissolving as much significance as you can, from your deep heart sincerely ask for appropriate guidance or insight. If you don't get an answer, find something to appreciate for a while.

Now it's your turn to practice the steps.

Step 1 — Be aware of how you feel about the issue at hand. Learn to observe and name your feelings. Be honest with yourself. Admitting how you feel is the first step in transformation. Most people notice thoughts constantly flitting through their minds. It's harder to notice feelings skimming under the surface. This is because emotions occur faster than thought, and faster than your mind's ability to intercept them. Many times, how you feel will be clear and easy to name: angry, anxious, overwhelmed, guilty, sad, happy, joyful, and so forth. Other times there may be confusing undercurrents of feelings. Just name whatever feelings you can.

On some issues you may have "numbed out" your feelings because you're busy. Or you don't want to become self-absorbed. Or you don't want to feel bad. Or you have too much past hurt to want to stay in touch with your feelings. The problem, as you learned in the last chapter, is that even if you try to ignore disturbed feelings or pretend they're not there, your subconscious emotional undercurrents stay absorbed in them. You can shove them aside, but they are still depleting your energy. So the first step of Cut-Thru, being aware of how you feel, is critical to the process of transforming anxiety.

Here's how Tracy completed step 1:

> *My issue is I have to give my employees performance evaluations next week. When the evaluation is "performance improvement needed," I begin to feel really anxious. I want to find a hole to crawl into. For days, I've been conjuring up all types of pictures of how it might go. (Maybe I should have been a movie producer!) Using step 1, I easily am able to recognize and label the feeling of anxiety; no Sherlock Holmes needed on this one!*

Write down your issue and how you feel about it on your Cut-Thru worksheet.

Step 2 — Center yourself by breathing in through the heart and out through the solar plexus. Breathe love and appreciation through this area for thirty seconds or longer to help anchor your attention there. Breathing in through the area of the heart and out through the solar plexus (located about four inches below the heart, just below the sternum) helps keep your emotional energies anchored or grounded. The solar plexus, like the heart, has its own little brain with neurons, neurotransmitters, and oscillating rhythms. When you experience a frightening situation, your brain tells the adrenal glands in this area to release stress hormones that prepare the body to fight or flee. Your stomach contains many sensory nerves that are stimulated by this chemical surge — hence the butterflies (Gershon 1999). That's why you feel sensations of anxiety or fear in the solar plexus area or get a knot in your stomach when you're upset.

Strong instincts also affect this gut brain, giving you gut feelings that tell you to take or avoid action. At times this sensation can be a helpful warning signal, but frequently it's an instinctual stop-go reaction that's not based in current reality. This is usually the case with overcare and anxiety. Many people confuse "gut feelings" with their heart, but in fact the gut brain is more instinctive than intuitive. It's your heart that provides sensitive intuition that brings understanding. When the gut brain synchronizes with the heart, you have more clarity and power.

Step 2 begins to bring the gut brain into synchronization with the heart. Breathing a positive feeling or attitude, like love or appreciation — in through the heart and out through the solar plexus — helps generate the coherent power needed to shift disturbed feelings toward a calmer state. How do you do this? Imagine breathing the positive feeling or attitude in through your heart, and exhaling out through your solar plexus to help anchor in the positive attitude. Don't stress about whether you are doing it right. Just practice this gently and sincerely. After thirty seconds or so, you may find your emotions shifting toward an easier or more pleasant state. Strong emotional reactions will need longer, especially if your issue is about a deep hurt. Be genuine and stay with it. If you have the time, practice step 2 for several minutes. If you can't find a feeling of love or appreciation, it's okay. Just breathe an attitude of appreciation for something—anything—to get back in sync. It's worth the effort. You will learn what being synchronized feels like.

Here's what happened when Tracy practiced step 2 on her issue:

> *Breathing appreciation for myself and my employee, in through the heart and out through the solar plexus, immediately calmed me and created more of a solid feeling inside.*

Write down what you feel and perceive from practicing step 2 on your Cut-Thru worksheet.

Step 3 — Assume objectivity about the feeling or issue — as if it were someone else's problem. Step 3 involves finding the maturity to disengage from an issue for a few moments in order to let the emotions release and come back to balance. You can pretend you are watching another person dealing with your issue. It's like looking at yourself from a distance or from the point of view of your higher self. This helps give you a more dispassionate and objective view. You might imagine yourself as another person sitting a few feet away or standing below you, as if you are watching this person from a helicopter or from a bird's-eye view. One of the first things you may notice is how much more compassionate and understanding you are toward this other person than you have been toward yourself. Compassion is a core heart feeling that also helps increase heart rhythm coherence and synchronization between the heart and brain.

Most of the time, when your emotions get hung up on an issue it's because you are overidentified or overattached. You get tangled up in it because at some level you believe that your identity or your fulfillment is at stake. You need to learn how to step back from the issue, to say, "I'm not the same as this problem," so that you can keep a more open mind about what is really happening. Marriage counselors and mediators spend about 80 percent of their time trying to get their clients to step back and see things more objectively. The same is needed when mediating a dispute within your own self. You'll never get anywhere if your mind is made up and your emotions are rigid.

Whatever you perceive in step 3, keep your attention and energy focused in the heart to stay in coherence. As an emotion or issue releases, you might feel it all over again—old perceptions, thoughts, and feelings spinning out from cellular storage. That's part of the process. Don't buy in to those feelings all over again. Hold to your objectivity whatever your feelings are doing. It can seem you're going backward, but you're not. It helps to remind yourself that it's just the accumulated anxiety spinning out.

If the emotions still overtake you, it's okay. Just go back to step 2 and breathe genuine care or compassion for yourself to regain your composure. Know that your root motive to care about the issue is right but that you're getting caught up again in the emotions surrounding the issue. Knowing this is caring for yourself. Have compassion for yourself that it's only human, but you don't have to stay there. You can Cut-Thru.

Step 3 helps you to step outside the maelstrom of emotions so that your common sense—your heart intelligence—can intuitively guide this other person, you, to appropriate action.

When Tracy applied step 3 to her issue on giving a less-than-stellar review to her employee, she found her perceptions began to shift:

> *When I looked at the situation as if it were someone else's problem, some clarity emerged. I needed to keep in mind how I would want to be communicated with if I were the one getting the review. I know that I would want to be told if I needed to make a change that would benefit my team, colleagues, or me. I bet my employee feels that way deep down, too. This was promising!*

Write down any shifts in perceptions or new ways to look at and address the issue after practicing step 3 on your Cut-Thru worksheet.

Step 4—Rest in neutral—in your rational, mature heart. By finding some objectivity, you get closer to a state of neutral and can rest in a more peaceful heart. Steps 1 through 3 help you become more neutral about issues that have strong negative emotional accumulation or "stacked stress." Being neutral doesn't mean that you have to agree with anything that happened. It simply means becoming neutral toward your uncomfortable feelings, thoughts, and memories about the issue. This gives you more power and reduces their energy drain.

Try to relax and ease feelings and thoughts that are not neutral into the heart. This allows the heart to transform incoherent emotional energy. It provides an opportunity for more peace and new possibilities to emerge. In some situations you may be assuming motives you don't know. In neutral you ask yourself, "What if there's something I don't know?" The attitude of "I don't really know" helps the mind become humble and open, so that heart intelligence can surface to show you a new perspective. Even if what happened was tough and you were hurt or traumatized, in neutral you can still ask yourself, "Haven't I drained enough from this? Isn't it time to at least try to neutralize the stored energies, to get on with my life?"

The rational mature heart is a place inside that is balanced in its attitudes. The balance provided by heart intelligence will allow your intuition to present you with commonsense go-forward strategies that are best for you and everyone involved.

Here's what happened to Tracy when she used step 4:

Resting in neutral, I found a peace here, but every few seconds I felt some of the old thoughts and feelings resurface, so I went back to breathing compassion through the heart and solar plexus to anchor myself back in the mature heart — a place where I could remain calm and objective.

Practice step 4, then write down your feelings and perceptions on your Cut-Thru worksheet. If you find that you were not able to remain neutral, don't worry. This is normal in learning how to Cut-Thru, especially if the issue has a lot of anxiety and emotional investment associated with it. You aren't bad. Just go back to step 2 for a few moments, like Tracy did, breathing compassion for yourself in through your heart and out through your solar plexus so you become more grounded. Then move through step 3 and step 4 again until you can rest in a more neutral, mature heart that is willing to say, "What if I wasn't bad?" or "What if I really don't have the whole picture?" or "It's time to forgive myself (or another) and move on" and mean it.

Steps 1 through 4 have prepared you for the last steps of the technique, which will help you to release an anxiety pattern at the neural-electrical and biochemical levels. As you practice steps 5 and 6, you clear out the residues and lay in a new pattern.

Step 5 — Soak and relax any disturbed or perplexing feelings in the compassion of the heart. Dissolve the significance a little at a time. Remember, it's not the problem that causes energy drain as much as the stored significance you have assigned to the problem. When you feel disturbed about something, realize *it's not the issue itself* that's causing you discomfort. It's the importance or emotional significance that you have invested in the issue. On major issues, it's nearly impossible not to have assigned a lot of significance. And that's all right. But now it's time to start anew. Knowing that stored significance will only keep on draining your energy, you can commit now more than ever to release it. In step 5, you use the coherent power of the heart to end this chapter in your life. Have respect for yourself and compassion for having gone through that experience. After all, you were hurt. Now it's time to release any self-judgments or feelings of having "done bad" in response to the situation. It's all okay. You can take a lot of significance out by knowing that many others would have reacted in the same way. This helps to more quickly forgive and release the issue within your system.

Through practicing step 5, you can let all that go and align yourself with a new commitment to move forward. What is important to your healing is your ability to keep your heart open and release the entrapments of what your mind is insisting should have happened instead. Soak any feeling of "poor me" out of your system. Being a victim doesn't serve you. It only keeps the same old feelings spinning round and round. You've already done this enough.

In step 5, you keep taking perplexing feelings and memories back to the heart and soaking them there to dissolve the significance. You keep relaxing resistances (pain or compressed or stuck energy) that you may be feeling in the heart. Just allow resistance or heaviness to simply soak in the energy of the heart. Don't worry if it doesn't release entirely. Feeling compassion for yourself will accelerate the process.

Take your time with this step. Emotional histories are deeply ingrained patterns in your neural circuitry and cells, which is why they keep resurfacing and taking hold of you. Depending on how deep these feelings go and how much reinforcement they've had, there may be a lot of emotional energy stored in them. As you dissolve the significance and transform the stored incoherent energy, you gradually release the pattern, resulting in more peace and satisfaction.

Tracy wrote the following after practicing step 5:

I began to relax more and was able to remove some of the significance that I had placed on the situation with my employee. It was now getting clear that my emotions were being fueled by not wanting to hurt another person's feelings. I did not want her to think I was bad or unhappy with her as a person. This was my own vanity and a common pattern in many areas of my life. That insight gave me some release. I felt calmer and more objective about the issue and realized I didn't need to take it personally. There simply needed to be an adjustment. I would tell her that the performance of her work tasks needed to improve and I would help in any way I could to facilitate that improvement. Whew! I began to feel more balanced

*even though I knew that I couldn't anticipate her
reaction to this news.*

Practice step 5, then write down your feelings and perceptions on your Cut-Thru worksheet. Assign unresolved
feelings to soak in the heart as you move on to step 6.

**Step 6 — After dissolving as much significance as you can,
from your deep heart sincerely ask for appropriate guidance or insight.** If you don't get an answer, find something to
appreciate for a while. Now, after having done steps 1
through 5, you are more able to hear your heart intelligence.
The heart doesn't always flash its answer on a neon sign. A
lot of times, heart intelligence comes to you softly and subtly.
When people talk about the "still, small voice" of the heart,
they are saying that the heart communicates through a deli-
cate intuitive feeling or subtle knowing. It's important to follow even fleeting heart perceptions. If a perception is
peaceful and feels good to you, that's your signal to follow it,
even if it seems too simple or easy.

Here's Tracy's experience with step 6:

*After I removed all the significance that I could feel
and think of, I sincerely asked my heart intelligence to
help me write the evaluation. I also asked for
instructions on how to proceed in the meeting. The
most difficult part was done — letting go of the anxiety
that kept me from moving forward effectively. Writing
the evaluation was a lot easier once I released the
anxious feelings. I knew intuitively what to write and
felt good about what I said. The review, although not
perfect, went smoother than I expected. We addressed
the issues and set new goals. She also agreed to do
some extra training, which she went ahead and took.*

Now practice step 6 and write your feelings and perceptions on your Cut-Thru worksheet. Don't despair if you don't get new intelligence on the spot. Sometimes you will draw a blank. That can be an indicator that the most helpful approach for now is to put the issue aside for a while and move on.

The most effective way to move on is to find something to appreciate. Take whatever glimmers of peace or release you have gained from Cut-Thru and appreciate them, or choose something in your life to appreciate. Appreciation helps sustain the coherence you have built and can keep you from being pulled as far back into old patterns. Intentionally generating appreciation often brings clarity on other issues you are working on, so it's a productive use of your time and energy. Use Attitude Breathing for thirty seconds or longer, breathing appreciation so you can rise above the issue you've been using Cut-Thru on and move on to something else. Allow insights to come to you later as you put your attention elsewhere.

Take Action

Remember to keep writing down any glimmers of new perceptions so you can remember them. If you don't act on your insights right away, they can fade or you can begin to doubt them. Put them into action and watch how things can improve.

To give you more sensitivity to how the Cut-Thru process works, read the "Inside the Cut-Thru Technique" section in chapter 6. Often just reading more about it helps people get more release.

Set a Practice Program

You'll be surprised at how many issues can be Cut-Thru in only a few sittings. Others will take time. Keep going for it. If you have difficulty, experiment with the order of the steps. Some people with traumatic or deeply charged issues find it helpful to first do steps 1 and 2, then steps 5 and 6, to increase coherence and dissolve significance so they can achieve a more objective, neutral understanding in steps 3 and 4. The tendency is to try to jump to a mind understanding without shifting enough underlying feeling into coherence so that intuition can come in.

Find a place where you can Cut-Thru with no interruptions or distractions from other people, telephones, or pets for ten to fifteen minutes (or less, if you arrive at your objective sooner). It doesn't take long to get a release or insight if you are in a peaceful and genuine frame of mind. Approach practice sessions with a genuine heart attitude, instead of trying to find a quick fix to get the monkey off your back. The latter won't give you the coherence you need to Cut-Thru.

Many people find it helpful to practice the Heart Lock-In technique, given in chapter 6, before their Cut-Thru practice. Heart Lock-In helps you find that more peaceful and genuine place. It helps you stay in your heart through locking into and sending positive attitudes to your feelings, your body, other people, or issues. Practicing Heart Lock-In for even five minutes will increase your power to sustain coherence and get back to coherence faster when you get out of balance. As you make genuine efforts to practice a more coherent, peaceful state, more of your real spirit can come in to help.

Practice Cut-Thru five days a week to build your coherence power. You can do it more often of course, but set yourself a goal and regular practice program and stick with it for a month. That's not a long time, considering how much more time you've invested in anxiety issues. Commitment to a Cut-Thru practice plan is an investment in yourself and in taking individual responsibility.

To make your practice simpler, you can tape-record the steps of Cut-Thru at a pace that feels right to you. Then, you can listen to the recording and guide yourself through the steps without getting distracted by reading them. Have a pencil and a Cut-Thru worksheet in front of you, and pause the recording to write down your feelings and perceptions after each step.

Create Cut-Thru Worksheets

Create Cut-Thru worksheets for your practice program. Divide a piece of paper or a page in your journal into six sections, one for each step or create several in your journal or notebook. Write down the heading or questions for each section as given in the box below and leave enough room between headings to write your answers. Make copies of the Cut-Thru worksheet. Write the date of each session to keep track of your progress and remind you of what your heart intelligence is showing you. Cut-Thru one issue at a time. If you can't formulate an issue, use anxiety, fear, or another stress feeling as your issue. If more issues pop up as you go through the steps, don't worry—that's part of the clearing process. Just keep going through the steps and following your heart.

Participants in a research study who practiced the Cut-Thru technique five days a week for thirty days experienced significantly reduced anxiety, guilt, burnout, stress, and hostility, along with significantly increased contentment, caring, warmhearted emotions, and vigor (McCraty, Barrios-Choplin, Rozman, et al. 1998). To facilitate your practice, you can do the steps while listening to Doc's music on the CD *Speed of Balance,* which was designed to facilitate emotional release from cellular patterns and regeneration and was used in the Cut-Thru study.

Cut-Thru Worksheet

Step 1. My issue

Step 2. Describe any shifts in feeling or perceptions after practicing step 2.

Step 3. What would I tell another person with this issue? Describe any subtle or obvious shift in perceptions after practicing step 3.

Step 4. What options do I see from a more neutral state? Describe any feeling or perception shifts from practicing step 4.

Step 5. On a scale of 1 to 10, how much significance have I invested in this issue? Describe any feeling or perception shifts after practicing step 5.

Step 6. Cut-Thru response. Feelings or insights that my heart intelligence is offering me.

Practice Makes Permanent

After some sessions of committed practice, you'll start to find the rhythm of the technique and how the six steps flow together energetically to give you release. Once you find the flow, the steps will be easier to use in shorter time periods. Eventually you'll be able to just use the Quick Cut-Thru Steps below to remind you of what to do. Many find it helpful to write the Quick Cut-Thru Steps on sticky notes and place them on their computer screen, bathroom mirror, or other convenient places. Alexis says, "Seeing and moving through the quick steps when I'm on the run and feeling anxious helps get my mind and heart working together. Usually I go through all six steps in a row, but sometimes my heart just pops in with one to use and it really helps."

Quick Cut-Thru Steps

Step 1. Be aware of how you feel.

Step 2. Breathe a positive feeling or attitude.

Step 3. Assume objectivity.

Step 4. Rest in neutral.

Step 5. Soak and relax.

Step 6. Ask for guidance; appreciate.

Practicing Cut-Thru is training in emotional strength and flexibility. You'll surprise yourself at how adept you can become at managing your emotional energy. You'll get release on issues that have been bothering you and find that you are re-creating your life. And you'll reach a place where some of those problems you've been working on and working out for a long time are finally coming to resolution.

chapter 5

Accelerated Clearing

The part can never be well unless the whole is well.

—Plato

The pace of life today is moving much faster than in previous eras and is continuing to speed up. This can cause anxiety when you feel you can't keep up. However, you can use the accelerating pace to your advantage to shorten the process of clearing. You can learn to shift emotions and attitudes faster as you ride the speed wave, instead of getting dragged down in the undertow. You can reach inside and find the power to change.

Challenges to Clearing

The biggest challenge in clearing is getting your emotions to agree with what you conceptually know is true. Despite your efforts, emotions can have their way with you, taking you back into the same old feelings and reactions, restocking and restoring significance. The quickest way to stop this is to clear as soon as anxiety triggers, before it starts a downward spiral and energy drain. In chapter 3 you learned Tools in Action to help clear overcare and anxiety as they come up in the moment.

If you let a downward spiral start, its energetic momentum can take you down into all the stored significance from the past. Then it feels like you have to fight your way out or climb your way out of the quicksand, if you can. In chapter 4 you learned the Cut-Thru technique to harness the power of your physiology and spirit to clear deeper issues and long-standing anxieties that have stored emotional significance. More understanding of how clearing works physiologically and energetically can speed up your process.

You Do Have Choice

You activate different heart rhythms and neural circuits based on choice. To shorten the process of clearing, you have to deepen your intention. What lengthens the process is not having a deep enough commitment to halt a downward spiral. This is why the tool Notice and Ease is so important. You have to recognize what's going on and ease in to the heart so that you *can* make a choice. The Power of Neutral tool is critical at that choice point. It allows your emotions to settle so you can make a conscious choice about which way to go. The Attitude Breathing tool then allows your heart and mind to shift into alignment to make a *heart-intelligent* choice. If anxiety still won't release, use the Cut-Thru technique or just the Quick Cut-Thru Steps. Soak and relax in the heart to allow the significance to dissolve. It doesn't take as much soak time these days to move the old out and get new clarity—another benefit of the accelerating pace of life.

> Bill describes the choice: "I easily fall into impatience and get overly demanding with my eight-year-old daughter.

*My body becomes rigid; my breath is shallow; my mus-
cles tighten."* Bill learned that he has a choice about
which emotional road to go down. *"I can stay impatient,
or I can immediately use a tool to go to my heart for
greater calmness. I have a choice as to what kind of a person I want to be. Would I rather be righteous and rigid,
or would I rather be happy, centered, grounded, and
joyful?"*

Getting Aligned Emotionally

It's easy to get inspired by insight but not have enough
committed intent to act on it. You have to take it to the street.
Intuition plus follow-through creates the energetic momentum you need for clearing old patterns.

Even when you get new clarity, you can still feel unsettled emotions that are not yet aligned with the heart. The
mind understands at a surface level. This is a conceptual
understanding but lacks emotional alignment, so it doesn't
have the power to clear.

Here's an example: Two people have an argument and
on the surface resolve the issue. Being decent human beings,
as they leave the room one checks in: "I'm okay. Are you
okay?" and the other says she's fine. But both leave with
unresolved feelings. When they see each other again there is
a distance between them because the unsettled emotions
didn't totally clear. They got conceptual agreement, but not
emotional agreement. There wasn't enough heart openness
and honesty to get the emotional clearing.

Right now, as you read these words, this is actually happening between millions of people all over the world. Most
know something is missing, but they don't know what to do.

They smile and say they're fine, but they don't have the alignment with the heart needed to find peace.

With conceptual alignment there can be only piecemeal peace within oneself, or between parents and children, spouses, or even nations. Countries can be aligned in their policies on the conceptual level, but not on the emotional level. This leads to ongoing distrust and erupts in conflicts.

People stay in therapy for years while their therapists try to help them address emotional issues with a practical conceptual approach. This rational approach often misses the emotional dynamics going on internally. If the therapist doesn't have enough alignment with the heart to know what is needed, the patient stays dismayed. This is why the heart is essential in therapy. The heart operates in a different energetic domain that has the power to align and untangle the emotions.

Jasmina Agrillo, a Licensed HeartMath Provider and stress management specialist, describes a profound clearing her client had using the Cut-Thru technique to release sexual trauma from her father and grandfather.

> *My client had arrived at a compassionate*
> *understanding of the patterns of suffering in her*
> *father's and grandfather's life that would cause them*
> *to sexually abuse her, but she couldn't experience*
> *release at the feeling level. Because of that, she was*
> *still reliving the trauma and living in fear. It took*
> *just two sessions with the Cut-Thru technique for her*
> *to come to a deep level of healing and peace she had*
> *never experienced before with any other process. Step*
> *5, soak and relax, and step 6, ask for guidance,*
> *empowered a deep cellular release from the experience*
> *and new understanding. Of her own volition, my*
> *client fully forgave her father and grandfather. It was*

a profound experience for me as a coach to witness the intelligent presence of Love or God that the heart brings in when we consciously light the spark of appreciation and real care.

The Physiology of Clearing

Emotions are electromagnetic and biochemical processes. Emotions also cause muscular reactions. Anxiety and frustration can tighten your neck and shoulders; fear can grip your heart or cause a churning in your stomach. By contrast, love, appreciation, and compassion can soothe and inspire you, allowing your muscles to smooth out and your organs to function with greater harmony and flow.

In addition to affecting muscular reactions, emotions create hormonal responses. Positive emotions create different hormonal responses than negative (stressful) emotions. Even feeling numb or feeling nothing are still emotional states that create hormonal responses. Over time, your hormonal responses become set patterns that in themselves start to trigger automatic emotional and physiological reactions that profoundly impact how you feel.

Emotions and Hormones

Hormones are chemical messengers that regulate many of your body's functions and affect the way your brain processes information. Hormones are found in the brain, heart, and throughout the body. How hormones work to condition how you feel is still being uncovered. In 1983, the heart was reclassified as part of the hormonal system when a new hormone produced by the heart was discovered (Cantin and Genest 1986). Nicknamed the "balance hormone," atrial natriuretic peptide (ANP) carries information throughout the body and has receptors in the blood vessels, kidneys, adrenal glands, and brain. ANP helps reduce the effects of stress. Recently, other hormones have been found to be produced in the heart in large quantities, including oxytocin, called the "love hormone" because it is secreted more during satisfying sex, social bonding, and by mothers at childbirth (Gutkowska et al. 2000).

The repeated experience of anxiety leads to a chronic elevation of the stress hormone cortisol, along with a reduction in DHEA (dehydroepiandrosterone), the vitality or anti-aging hormone. The cortisol-to-DHEA ratio is often considered a biological marker of stress and aging.

Cortisol levels go up when you feel negative emotions or stress. Cortisol levels go down when you feel positive emotions such as appreciation, care, and love. Too much cortisol impairs immune function, triggers excessive fat buildup around the waist and hips, decreases bone and muscle mass, impairs memory and learning, destroys brain cells, and ages you before your time (Guyton 1991; Sapolsky 1992). Too much cortisol over long periods resets your body's thermostat. Your brain thinks higher cortisol is the norm and continues to produce more than it needs. This makes it harder to wind down and relax or release anxiety.

DHEA has the opposite effect from cortisol. DHEA is the most prolific hormone in the body and is the hormone that many other hormones are made from, including testosterone and estrogen. Scientists have linked reduced levels of DHEA with exhaustion, depression, immune disorders, fertility and menstrual problems, Alzheimer's, heart disease, obesity, and diabetes. High levels of DHEA can produce increased feelings of general well-being and enhanced vitality

(Shealy 1995). As you clear negative emotions from your system, your body produces less cortisol and more DHEA.

Using tools and techniques to shift into a more positive emotional state will change your hormonal state. Then your hormones start working for you and add to the energetic momentum of clearing and renewal. In one study of participants practicing the Cut-Thru technique, cortisol levels were reduced an average of 23 percent while DHEA levels increased by over 100 percent in just thirty days of practice (McCraty, Barrios-Choplin, Rozman, et al., 1998).

The Amygdala and Stored Significance

For decades scientists thought all sensory information went first to the brain's neocortex (thinking center), where it was conceptually understood; and only then to the amygdala (part of the emotional center), where an emotional response was added. Now research shows that the amygdala can initiate an emotional response even before your neocortex has a chance to consider the situation. That's why people so often feel and react before they think (LeDoux 1996).

In other words, before you can even think, your amygdala is reacting to and evaluating life emotionally. The amygdala stores strong emotional experiences from your past that have significance to you. It assigns current significance and meaning to your life experiences based on previous emotional experience. According to Dr. Jonathan Bargh, a psychologist at New York University, "It is emotion that decides for the brain and body the value of information being processed" (quoted in Goleman 1995). This is why you can have conceptual understanding but not emotional agreement.

The amygdala constructs reality based on emotional patterning from the past, which colors your current perceptions and reactions. Strong emotional experiences become your body's emotional history. These emotional histories will condition how you feel and react to situations now. You can be operating like a split screen, your rational or conceptual mind saying one thing and your feelings another because of stored emotional histories.

For instance, if a dog snarled at you when you were two years old and it caused a strong feeling of fear, your amygdala may send out panic messages even when you encounter a friendly dog now. If you opened your heart to someone in the past, and after an initial period of warmth and intimacy, ended up feeling hurt and betrayed, your amygdala's response to initial feelings of intimacy now might be fear and an instinct to close off your heart. Even after you feel you have released the hurt, just seeing the person who hurt you can again trigger the emotional significance that was stored.

The neural connections going from the amygdala to the neocortex are stronger and more plentiful than the wiring going the other direction (LeDoux 1996). Nature designed people this way as a strong survival mechanism. That's why people are often tempted to believe that they have no control over strong emotional reactions. But when it comes to getting along with others and freeing themselves from emotional histories that get in the way, they need to release themselves from the clutches of the amygdala. Since emotional processes can work faster than thought, it takes a power stronger than thought to override them. It takes the power of the heart.

Heart Coherence Changes the Amygdala

As your heart rhythm pattern changes, so does the electrical activity in the cells of the amygdala. In fact, the cells in the amygdala synchronize to your heartbeat (Frysinger and

Harper 1990). Clearing techniques, tools, and therapies work faster when they introduce coherent rhythmic patterns from the heart to disrupt dysfunctional patterns stored in the brain. This changes your body's biochemistry as well. This is how emotional patterns, like fear or anxiety, can be cleared through the coherent power of your heart.

The Energetic Process of Clearing

Human beings are geniuses at creating and storing emotional histories. They are novices at learning how to get out of their entrapment. Negative emotional histories keep coming up as ankle biters to pull people back just when they are trying to see from new perspectives. These negative histories are like carrying a backpack full of rocks that weigh you down and tire you out. Nature designed human beings to store emotional histories for self-protection. Yet nature also provided the keys to emotional freedom. Once you find the keys, you have to unlock the door. The lock is your heart and the keys are your tools to open your heart.

You have to put the key in the lock and turn it to open the door to your heart's coherent power. It's the heart's coherent rhythms that bring in the power of your real self and your spirit to clear emotional histories. Since the heart is the strongest rhythmic oscillator in the body, it pulls the body's other rhythms into synchronization or entrainment with its own. The Cut-Thru technique will help create an energetic alignment with your heart.

Through using the tools and techniques, you start to change your physiology to work for you. Here's what another therapist wrote:

> *My last two clients who learned the Cut-Thru technique both had anxiety/worry issues. Both*

experienced significant relief from their issues and are now able to remain calm and balanced more often in their day. They expressed sincere gratitude to have gained control of their anxiety and worry. One also has a chronic illness (emphysema), chronic bronchitis, and diabetes. Her anxiety can easily trigger an emphysema attack requiring medication to come out of. She has now gained control of her anxiety to the extent she is able to go days without any medication for emphysema. The other client has been able to go off blood pressure medication. This is what Cut-Thru can do, not just emotionally but physically.

Getting the Amygdala to Work for You

By using the Tools in Action and Cut-Thru technique *now*, you can start to create for yourself positive emotional history going forward. Positive emotional histories that facilitate improved quality of life and health also get processed in the amygdala. Michael tells a story about his eighty-year-old parents:

Friday night was always a special time for my father and mother. They'd relax, allow themselves an extra cocktail, and enjoy a fun evening with friends or family. Now, fifteen years after retirement, the workweek agenda is no longer there. They could easily do on Monday what they do on Saturday. Yet they both exclaim how a buoyant-feeling memory magically returns every Friday night just as strong as it was in the midst of my father's career. Friday nights still feel very special and fun, just as they always did. I think it helps keep them healthy.

Make the choice to align your emotions with your heart, and you will set in place emotional patterns that will support you as you move forward in life. More of your real spirit comes in when your mind, emotions, and body are in alignment with your heart.

Taking Responsibility

You can empower yourself to take individual responsibility for clearing and move forward even if it's just one small step at a time. Small steps are large steps when you're talking about clearing emotions and issues that stifle your spirit and prevent inner peace.

As time and events continue to speed up, your emotions will keep speeding up too. Ride the wave of positive emotional shifts and you can accelerate clearing. Really wanting that—and committing to practice—is real self-care. The energetic and physiological process of clearing will become increasingly automatic as you practice. Sharon's story illustrates.

> *I inherited several generations of fear and depression from both sides of my family. I carried this in various forms of stress throughout my forty-nine years, resulting in physical and emotional imbalances. During my first Cut-Thru practice, I was able to see my fear as something ancient that I have outgrown and can leave behind me. This felt insight allowed me to drop a history of fear. And it stayed gone completely for a week. Absolute magic.*

But Sharon was not out of the woods.

> *The pattern peeked back in upon awakening one morning. Just a touch of the familiar panic. I*

*recognized it, admitted it, and proceeded with the
steps of Cut-Thru. I got a much more enjoyable start
to my day, but then the next morning the panic came
back again, although less than before. I was able to
soak out the anxiety and depression before I got out of
bed. I'm doing this every morning as I awake and feel
that I am holding strong with my intent and a new
appreciation of myself. I am creating a fresh
interpretation of me and of the world.*

Even more, Sharon is releasing and extinguishing the
pattern of fear and depression that she has at the cellular
level. Sharon says,

*I am confident that, with perseverance, I can continue
to disbelieve my fear until it will no longer find a
hold in me. Cut-Thru literally cut through my
internal prison.*

Her story shows that people can clear familiar patterns
of fear and anxiety that no longer serve them. Some emotional issues can be cleared very quickly, while others laden
with significance will take more time.

The poet Rainer Maria Rilke advised us to be patient
towards what is unresolved. He went even further and bid us
to love our questions themselves (Rilke 1993). Developing
emotional alignment with your heart intelligence provides
answers to the why questions. By using the tools and
Cut-Thru technique, you will develop resilience to stop going
around the same old circuits, and your physiology will
respond accordingly. Appreciate the process, and you will
find that you are re-creating your life with more happiness
and peace.

chapter 6

The Extraordinary Power of Coherence

The higher order of logic and understanding that is capable of meaningfully reflecting the soul comes from the heart.

—Gary Zukav, *Seat of the Soul*

Psychophysiological coherence is a scientific term that describes a highly efficient, health-promoting state associated with positive emotion and a high degree of mental and emotional stability. In other words, there is heart alignment between your mental, emotional, and physical systems, reflected by heart rhythm coherence. This is a natural human state that can occur spontaneously, but sustained periods are generally rare (McCraty and Childre 2004; McCraty et al. 2005).

Research shows that people can learn to sustain extended periods of psychophysiological coherence by generating positive emotions. Intentionally generating positive emotions to sustain coherence creates dynamic positive changes in the patterns of information flowing from your heart to your higher brain centers. This, in turn, makes it easier to sustain heart alignment and emotional stability for longer periods, even during challenging situations (McCraty et al. 2005; McCraty 2006).

Tests show that people who have regularly practiced HeartMath tools for a time start to exhibit more spontaneous periods of coherence in their heart rhythms throughout a day, even without any intentional effort to generate that state. They find themselves moving in a state of intuitive flow more consistently (McCraty and Childre 2004). Observed outcomes in laboratory, workplace, educational, and clinical studies include reduced stress, anxiety, and depression; decreased burnout and fatigue; enhanced immunity and hormonal balance; improved cognitive performance; and health improvements in a number of clinical populations (McCraty, Atkinson, and Tomasino 2001; McCraty and Childre 2004).

The Power of Coherence

In nature, the power of coherence cannot be underestimated. For example, coherent laser light is far more powerful than incoherent light from an ordinary lightbulb. This is because the photons are in alignment and not scattered. Stanford University materials science professor emeritus Dr. William Tiller tells us, "The shift from incoherence to coherence can bring such dramatic effects that if the light waves from a sixty-watt lightbulb could be made as coherent as a laser, it would become equivalent to a million or more watt bulb." Dr. Tiller goes on to say, "By the same principle, heart rhythms that are coherent can more powerfully impact the mind, emotions, and body than heart rhythms that are incoherent and chaotic. This understanding that we can intentionally harness the power of the heart brings great hope for the healing of humanity." Coherence-generating techniques help people harness that power to heal psychological trauma and transform hurt and pain.

Transforming Hurt

An important benefit of coherence techniques is that they bring laserlike power to your real care and love to repair psychological damage from situations in which you felt deeply hurt or betrayed. The coherence of the heart can mend a broken heart. Often anxiety disorders originate from or are triggered by traumatic relationship experiences. Not getting what you wanted or needed emotionally from someone you loved or relied upon can trigger a deep fear and anxiety about your self-worth. Closing down the heart is a natural defense mechanism when you have been hurt. But you have to walk through that doorway of defense to reclaim your emotional power. You have to open your heart to yourself. Many don't want to open their heart to deeper feelings because they are afraid they'll get swept back into the pain.

"My heart is what gets me into trouble," some people say. They believe the heart isn't trustworthy. The heart gets blamed because their genuine love or care became compromised by emotional attachment or expectation. Understandable as that may be, especially between parents and children or between mates, it's the emotional attachment or expectation that gets broken, not your real heart. The brain sends out distress signals, and you feel the pain of hurt, rejection, or betrayal in the heart.

Even in the midst of emotional pain, some love or care can still be flowing toward the person who hurt you, unless you've totally shut down your heart. That's where love can get so confusing. Once your heart starts to shut down, the mind takes over with feelings of being owed, anger, resignation, and anxiety. The heart and mind struggle, and this can result in an anxiety disorder or depression.

Being Heart Vulnerable

The coherence tools and techniques are designed to compassionately guide you through the process of healing. It starts with reopening your heart.

You become heart vulnerable as you open to your feeling world and what's really going on inside. Heart vulnerability is not being emotionally weak or sentimental or opening yourself to criticism or attack. Heart vulnerability requires strength to be honest with yourself about whatever you are feeling. Tremendous energy is locked up in feelings. Honestly acknowledging what's going on allows trapped emotional hurt to release. Admitting what you're feeling opens you to your authentic power and to the wisdom of your heart.

Heart vulnerability starts by making a listening agreement with yourself—that you will listen more honestly to your feelings. This is not a posture you assume; it's simply an agreement to listen more deeply to your own heart. Start with simple, everyday situations. Focus your energies in your heart and ask yourself, "What am I really feeling about this upcoming conversation, a meeting that's been dragging on and on, or the way my son rudely spoke to my wife?" Is it hurt, anger, boredom, confusion? This allows you to become aware of undercurrents that may be motivating your choices without your knowing it.

Notice and Ease any anxiety or stress you may be feeling, and listen to your heart for intuitive direction. Anne Marie describes how using the simple tool Notice and Ease has helped her stay connected with her authentic power and creative flow:

> *During the day I frequently stop and use Notice and Ease as a personal check-in. Sometimes I see that I'm in my head with too many thoughts or pushing too hard or that I have a nagging worry that needs attention. Other times I discover I have feelings of joy I was not fully appreciating. Quite often Notice and Ease is all I need to shift to my heart, ease out the stress and anxiety, and feel better.*

Most people tend to notice other people's feelings and actions before they notice their own. It's easy to become preoccupied with what others did or didn't do, projecting anxiety about why they are that way. This only deflects your responsibility for your own feelings and energy. Use Notice and Ease to remain connected to and responsible for your own emotional energies.

If you don't realign your emotional energies with the heart as you go through the day, you store negative reactions that drain you. Once your energy is drained, the unhealed hurt and pain from old emotional histories can resurface. Use Notice and Ease, and be heart vulnerable with yourself. Use Power of Neutral and Attitude Breathing to bring in coherence to continue the healing process. Listen to your heart for insight and direction.

Some emotional reactions are stubborn and difficult to release on the run. When you can't clear the stress with one of the Tools in Action or when hurt or pain from an emotional history resurfaces, stop and use Cut-Thru for a few minutes. If the Quick Cut-Thru Steps aren't enough, take a ten-minute break to go through the Cut-Thru technique, or use it later when you have time to be alone and collect yourself.

Inside the Cut-Thru Technique

When you release blocked emotional energy, you might find that long-held hurt, trauma, resentment, or guilt can produce a few tears as stored significance and negative feelings leave your system. That's really okay. It's part of the process. If blame and sadness take over, *realize it's just the stored feelings spinning out of your system.* It doesn't mean that you're not making progress. Just hold to your intent. A few tears from the heart as feelings release are much different from the kind of crying that has a lot of pouting and self-pity mixed in. Disappointment can produce a little crying as the feelings release, or it can become a total tantrum when you cannot let go of what you wanted. Breathe neutral, rest in neutral, and hold a bottom line. Treat yourself firmly but gently, like you would a child whose tantrum finally wears out if the bottom line is held firmly. Realize it's just old feelings releasing. Hold to neutral about *whatever* you are feeling. This takes practice, especially when emotions are heaving. It helps to remember that these old feelings are not the real you.

If you have lived with feeling hurt or disappointed for a long time, tell yourself those emotions have had their time. Soak them in the heart, and take the significance out. Otherwise, hurt and resentful energies will dampen your spirit and enjoyment in life. Accept that whatever happened, you did the best you knew at that time. You may know this conceptually, but healing involves bringing your emotions into alignment with what you know. As stored significance releases, the set pattern unravels, providing insight into unsolved mysteries of your emotional history. New intuitive understandings will surface that can wipe away years of stress and disappointment. As stored stress leaves your system, peace returns. Hold to any peace you find, even if it is not a complete peace. Emotional freedom is achieved in stages. With Cut-Thru practice you will build the emotional energetic alignment you need to move on.

A health professional wrote this case study:

A client who experiences severe anxiety, obsessive compulsive behaviors, mood fluctuation, and sleeping difficulties has been learning how to use the HeartMath tools for the past three months. Initially she did not recognize any anxiety and could not respond to the techniques. Her breathing pattern was shallow, inconsistent and when she would attempt to relax she would automatically go into an anxiety response. Through consistent efforts, "baby steps," she was able to successfully experience the Cut-Thru process yesterday. She phoned this evening to inform me that the session was transformational. She explained that the experience was amazing and that the calm lasted for a long time. She wasn't tired during the day and today when she became anxious she did some of the steps and was able to maintain a calm state. Though she was taking medication, she acknowledged that the medication has not helped with anxiety reduction; rather it has helped with just her awareness of being anxious. Cut-Thru was the technique that allowed her to reduce the overwhelming impact that anxiety has on her ability to function. She has remained relaxed, aware, and able to manage her daily tasks for over twenty-four hours, without going into emotional overload or anxiety. This is a

fifty-four-year-old woman who has always been highly
anxious and impulsive! This is grand stuff.

Listening Sincerely

Whatever happens during your Cut-Thru practice, appreciate any progress, however small, and keep asking your heart for guidance. The heart's intuitive signal is often weaker than the mind at first, so you have to listen carefully and sincerely. The mind sometimes tries to jump in and mask the voice of the heart with "yeah, but," especially when the answer isn't something the mind wants to hear. Heart intuition can also work the other way and be loud and clear. Respect both ways, and realize that the process of learning to listen to the heart takes refinement.

You won't always get an "aha" right away or even the same day. Intuition can come when you least expect it, often after letting go of the issue and moving on. Some of the best insights occur not while tussling with an issue, but after the fact, while in the shower, taking a walk, or enjoying nature. That's why people tell each other to "sleep on it." Now scientists know that during deep sleep more coherence naturally comes in to the heart's rhythms. That's why people sometimes wake up with intuitive clarity.

Your heart intelligence may prompt you to talk with a friend or counselor or even to talk to the person you've had problems with. This requires courage. When it's someone whose love or approval you want, use Attitude Breathing of compassion to help overcome fear of rejection or of being judged. Be heart vulnerable and speak genuinely. If their response isn't helpful, just breathe neutral in the heart. Keep using the tools and listening to your heart. As you bring more heart into your interactions, you bring in more of your spirit to facilitate healing.

Getting What You Really Want

Realize that now, in this moment of time, you are creating. You are creating your next moment based on what you are feeling, thinking, and doing. You can let go of the belief that staying upset about the past or fearful of the future will somehow protect you. It requires emotional alignment with your heart to know what *your heart* really wants. Heart vulnerability, really wanting to know, and commitment to practice will help draw that out.

> *Kara entered a period in her life when everything seemed to be falling apart around her. Feelings of worthlessness and anxiety preoccupied her. Kara learned and began applying Cut-Thru to what she called "the layered silt of my feeling world." It was during her very first Cut-Thru practice that she came to know in her deepest being that she was not her old patterns.*
>
> *"It was when I used the objectivity step," Kara says, "I saw clearly, as on a movie screen, the patterns of worthlessness built over years that were embedded in my neurons and how I had identified 'self' as those patterns. In this moment I could see clearly that these were not who I really was. Checkmate."*
>
> *Kara then began to ask deeply, "If I am not my life-long patterns of thought and feeling, then what am I?" Immediately, she felt buoyancy, a feeling of fullness in the area around her heart, "a joyfulness so profound that it can't be completely expressed. I breathed through my*

heart and solar plexus to anchor these feelings of my real self."

Since then, nothing has been quite the same for Kara. "I can no longer pretend, for very long, that I am a victim of my old feeling patterns. I have experienced the difference and know that I have the choice to go to my heart or not, to be alive or to diminish myself by identification with what is not real. I am so much larger than a set of biochemical patterns that don't serve me. It's no longer acceptable to me to sit in the cloud of my old feelings, because I know what the other side feels like. There's no contest."

Many times since her initial breakthrough, Kara admits, she has sunk beneath the waves of emotion. "But kind of like a beach ball, I'm not down long before the buoyancy of my heart pops me through again. I remember, daily, that disturbed emotional patterns are only feelings that are out of coherence with my heart and to which I have added significance. I made them 'real' by adding the significance over the years, so I regularly take the significance out when the remnants of those patterns come back up."

Heart Lock-In

Heart Lock-In is an emotion restructuring technique that helps you sustain coherence for longer periods. It helps you establish, or lock in, new patterns. Most people find that practicing the Heart Lock-In technique in a quiet place for five minutes or more a couple times a day helps to accumulate energy and recharge their emotional system. This cushions the impact of day-to-day stress or anxiety. When stress or anxiety comes up, many find they can maintain heart focus, make clearer decisions, and dramatically reduce personal energy drain.

The Heart Lock-In Technique

Step 1. <u>Shift</u> your attention to the area of your heart and breathe slowly and deeply.

Step 2. <u>Activate</u> and sustain a genuine feeling of appreciation or care for someone or something in your life.

Step 3. <u>Send</u> these feelings of care toward yourself and others. This benefits them and especially helps recharge and balance your own system.

When you catch your mind wandering during a Heart Lock-In, don't worry. As soon as you notice, simply refocus your attention on the heart area and reconnect with a feeling of real care or appreciation. As you sustain coherence for five minutes or more in a Heart Lock-In, it makes the state more familiar and accessible when you need it to meet the challenges of stress. With practice, the coherent state becomes your new reference point. This makes the process of connecting with it more automatic. Practicing the Heart Lock-In technique while listening to background music that lifts your spirit can increase its positive effects (McCraty et al. 1996; McCraty, Barrios-Choplin, Atkinson, et al., 1998; McCraty, Atkinson, and Tomasino 2001).

If anxiety or concerns keep pulling you into the head during a Heart Lock-In, just keep bringing your focus back to the heart. As you keep pulling your attention back to the heart, you build your power to stay in heart coherence. Send care, compassion, or forgiveness into your heavy feelings to bring more coherence to them. You may not even know why a heavy or stuck feeling is there. That's standard until you unlock the emotional history underlying it. Don't let it weigh you down if it won't go away. Befriend the feeling and send compassion to help release the blockage. Resistant feelings come and go and are released gradually as you gain more heart intuition about them.

After your Heart Lock-In, write down ideas you'd like to remember to put into action. Continue to practice the Heart Lock-In technique to help you sustain the courage to carry out your intentions.

When to Practice Heart Lock-In

One of the most effective times to practice Heart Lock-In is first thing in the morning, to set the tone for the day. It will help you stay coherent in the midst of typical reoccurring stressors, such as getting ready for work, getting the kids off to school, dealing with traffic, and other challenging situations. Remember the underlined key words of each step—"Shift, Activate, Send"—and you're on your way.

Doing a short, midday Lock-In is very effective for off-setting the afternoon drag and reenergizing the emotional system. When your emotions are spent, it causes "afternoon slump." Afternoon slump results in less focus and low motivation, which can lead to anxiety.

Another time to use Heart Lock-In is just before sleep. Many people have found that practicing the Heart Lock-In technique before going to sleep promotes a more restful sleep and is especially helpful with insomnia.

Bringing in Your Spirit

Heart Lock-In brings in more of your spirit to help you sustain coherence and alignment between your spirit, emotions, mind, and body. As such, it can facilitate Cut-Thru and any other practice you do, like prayer, meditation, and affirmations, or act as a booster to other self-help or healing methods. Because coherent heart energy is so laserlike, building coherence with Cut-Thru then sustaining it with Heart Lock-In helps to accelerate healing. The more you sustain the coherence mode, the faster your brain's neural circuits may be retrained to operate from a healthier baseline. You can use Cut-Thru and Heart Lock-In together in one session to power up more coherence. Practice Cut-Thru and then do a Heart Lock-In and send appreciation. Many psychologists find Cut-Thru combined with Heart Lock-In a useful adjunct to therapy.

Dr. Pamela Aasen, a clinical psychologist, comments,

> *I tell patients that Heart Lock-In is like taking your daily vitamins for increased health. It decreases negative transference, and keeps the power with the client rather than with the doctor or psychologist. When I do a Heart Lock-In with clients, not only do they get relief, but also I see more ways to help them. Sometimes a lot of emotions come up because they are feeling safe enough to allow the feelings to resurface. Afterwards, they always report feeling better. With Heart Lock-In or Cut-Thru, some people think they're being told they shouldn't cry, be angry, or whatever. But that's not the case. What these tools help patients see is they can allow the feelings to come up and release without having to stay in these states endlessly. The tools help them rebuild their faith in themselves.*

chapter 7

Managing Overwhelm

The mass of men lead lives of quiet desperation.

— Henry David Thoreau

Many people experience unremitting overwhelm at work, and at home, day after day. They wonder how to navigate through it all. They soldier on because they have to and worry it's going to be this way forever. One executive was serious when he told his peers, "Only the dead have done enough." Chronic overwhelm is one of the major causes of anxiety and anxiety disorders.

When you're overwhelmed, your mind overloads with all that's going on. Your feelings get jerky, reactive, and irritable. This drains energy like a sieve, until you're dragging yourself around in fatigue. Overwhelm takes a toll on your nervous system, your immune system, and your hormonal system. Your body has to pay. Overwhelm makes you more susceptible to disease and speeds up the aging process.

Too many are on this downward spiral and just don't know how to reverse it. By increasing heart rhythm coherence and managing emotional drain, you increase *resilience*.

Resilience is the ability to bounce back fast from mental, emotional, or physical energy drains. Anyone can stop the overwhelm momentum without sacrificing getting things done or advancing in their career.

Overwhelm Tools

As soon as you feel the strain of too many things hitting at once, use the Power of Neutral tool to step back and reduce the emotional charge. Then, to increase heart rhythm coherence, breathe ease and calm while telling yourself to take the significance out of whatever is going on. Let it all go while you're doing the Attitude Breathing. Using these overwhelm tools only takes a few minutes, but you have to really *do* it, not try halfway while your mind is thinking about what you haven't gotten done yet. Keep breathing the attitude of ease and calm or breathe balance as you move through your activities to prevent overwhelm from coming back.

Dan says of his experience,

> *When I'm going too fast, it's usually because I'm trying to get something over with so I can get on to something I'd rather be doing. That's when I get into overload. I move too quickly and get ahead of myself, maybe spill something or have to do something twice. Now, when I see myself going too fast, I try to remember to get back in my heart to check in earlier. I use Attitude Breathing of ease and calm and then listen to my heart. Sometimes my heart tells me to stop and do what I'd rather be doing, then come back and finish the other task later. Other times, I need to finish what I'm doing first, but just making peace with that allows me to do better and enjoy it more.*

Accessing your heart intelligence will save you time and energy at any moment. Overwhelm tends to skew your choices for what to do or say next. Using one tool to transform overwhelm can stop a chain reaction of choices that would lead to wasted time or create situations that you later regret. Heart coherence clears the static from your mental screen and allows new possibilities. Don't think you've blown it if you forget to use a tool. Even if you've slid right into a full-blown case of panic, use a tool *then*. Soon you'll remember to transform overwhelm at earlier stages in the chain reaction.

Overwhelm and Your Nervous System

Overwhelm unattended will produce cycles of anxiety, fatigue, and temporary despair, so it's important to address it. The nervous system will keep sending you messages in the form of symptoms, trying to tell you to make a shift in self-care to recoup lost energy. After sustained bouts, the symptoms can become chronic.

If you continue to drive yourself after your emotional reserves become exhausted, you end up running on "raw nerve" energy. That's when you finally know you're on edge or tell others that your nerves are frayed or fried. It feels like electricity is coursing through your system without enough coating on the wires. Or it can feel like a short circuit is going on. As emotional energy gets exhausted, your brain can't function properly, and you see no way out. You need to renew your emotional buoyancy so that proper communication can flow through your neural networks.

✒ *Symptoms of Overwhelm*

The first step in transforming overwhelm is to recognize the symptoms. Check which symptoms apply to you:

- ○ *Time pressure: always rushed, too much to do, not enough time*

- ○ *Mentally scattered, not feeling in control*

- ○ *Tunnel vision: irritation at anyone or anything that breaks your focus*

- ○ *Internal pressure: raw or gnawing feeling in your gut, knot in your stomach*

- ○ *Impatience: lack of compassion for self and others, judgmental thinking*

- ○ *Feeling a constant slow burn inside*

- ○ *Low-grade shock and strain*

- ○ *Zombielike numbness: no feelings, positive or negative; mental or emotional paralysis*

- ○ *Feeling disconnected from life*

- ○ *Decreased enjoyment of projects, relationships, or life in general*

- ○ *Feeling all-consuming alarm and dread*

Once you've identified the symptoms, don't feel bad. Realize that overwhelm is a planetary ailment. Millions experience these symptoms and don't have tools to help them.

Common Causes of Overwhelm

The next step in transforming overwhelm is to identify the causes of your overwhelm so you know clearly when to use the tools.

Project Identity

One of the chief contributors to overwhelm is project identity. You invest mental energy in a project—and, maybe without realizing it, a lot of emotional energy too. All that energy going into one project can create tunnel vision, blocking out other important things in your life. It's a rare person who has never suffered from project identity. A key symptom is when you find yourself feeling irritated, anxious, or frustrated if anything or anyone interferes with the project you are focused on. This can occur especially when you're up against the wall with deadlines. Many people believe they have to push everyone away to press on. If this happens regularly, then project and relationship quality can suffer.

Overwhelm can also be triggered when you get steeped in a project that is taking longer than you thought it would. The mind sees too many other things to do that seem important. This creates time pressure, overload, and eventually overwhelm. You know it's tipped into overwhelm if you have undercurrents of negative self-talk or negative projections about others. It's important to see what's driving your project identity.

> *Haley's job responsibilities had increased tremendously. When a large and detailed project with a critical timetable was put on her plate, she knew it was going to take a concerted effort to keep her balance. Then another huge project was loaded on, right on top of the first one. Haley was overwhelmed. "I felt intense anxiety mounting inside*

me," she said. "I felt I was going to explode, not from anger but from being pumped with stress. I thought desperately, 'This is only the third day into the launch, and I've got six more weeks!'" Every time someone would ask her a question, Haley felt something locking up inside.

Haley decided she needed to use the Cut-Thru technique to get to the bottom of it. After spending ten minutes on a break with the technique, Haley realized her project identity wasn't about a sense of accomplishment, as she'd thought. Underneath was a running sense of being "not good enough." "This surprised me," said Haley. "If I could juggle numerous balls in the air at once, somehow I thought this would make me a better human being. Once I began to dissolve the significance, it put things in perspective. I had to admit that it just wasn't possible for one person to handle everything on my plate. In fact, it was a joke. In taking the significance out and finding humor in the situation, I was finally able to see what I could let go of."

If you multitask and shift focus or concepts too often, it puts a strain on the heart, brain, and body, which haven't had time to sync up. Then, if even one or two concept shifts are accompanied by a negative emotion of irritation or frustration, the body goes into a stress response, releasing cortisol and other stress hormones. This can create an emotional dryness you become so used to that it feels normal. Many have forgotten how much better life could feel.

To address project identity — or any overidentity with issues, people, or situations that cause overwhelm — practice the overwhelm tools described above using Power of Neutral and Attitude Breathing, and keep telling yourself to take the significance out. Use these tools on both the small stuff and on mental states that preoccupy you during the day. Make note of what really is just "the small stuff" and what's the deeper stuff that you need to address with Cut-Thru practice. Taylor wrote,

> *My usual 3:00 P.M. mental state is too much to do, not getting things done fast enough, and feeling used up with hours to go before the workday will be over. Through practicing the Cut-Thru technique, I got to a place where I understood it was my perception of too much to do that was causing me more drain than the number of projects. Then I realized I had to go past conceptually knowing this and use the overwhelm tools in real time to keep this perspective during the day.*
>
> *My projects are still abundant, but my attitude has changed. I may feel a little tired sometimes, but an increasing ease from not putting so much significance on everything has improved both my outlook and my efficiency. I've come to see that so much of what I was putting significance on didn't really warrant it.*

Reasons That Drive Too Much Significance

The mind usually assigns too much significance for one or more of the following reasons:

- Overcare: *"I have to take care of everyone and everything, because no one else will."*

- Future projections, worst-case scenario: *"If I don't do it all, I could lose my job."*

- Approval needs: *"This is an important project that makes me important."* Or *"Anyone who can handle this much responsibility is more valuable."*

- Comparisons: *"Everyone else is overwhelmed, so I have to be or I won't measure up."*

- Ambition: *"I've got to get it done to get what I want."* Or *"I've got to have what I want to be happy, and I'll do anything to get it."*

- Good that gets in the way: *"I'm a good person to work so hard."*

- Performance anxiety: *"If I don't get it right or don't do well enough, I won't be liked."*

Do you see yourself in any of the above examples? Write the reasons behind your overwhelm in your journal. Use them as issues in your Cut-Thru practice.

Ann identified performance anxiety behind her overwhelm. When her boss asked her if there was anything he needed to know, she felt a tightening in her solar plexus. Her thoughts raced, "Doesn't he know I haven't had time to prepare?" and she was overcome by a strong feeling of anxiety. Ann answered feebly, and he said they'd talk later. As she walked away she told herself, "Just eeease, breathe balance, take the significance out." Within a few moments her attitude shifted as she realized she'd overpersonalized his question. Intuitively she knew everything was fine; he was genuinely asking the question and didn't mean to put any pressure on her. Ann remarked, "It was amazing how a river of intuitive knowing came in that transformed my performance anxiety within minutes."

Telling yourself to take the significance out with genuine intent is especially powerful when you tend to be overly self-conscious or keep running over social interactions in your mind after the fact or always wonder if you said or did the right thing. Taking significance out helps ease things back to their proper balance and proportion. Then your heart intelligence and intuition can get through.

Information Overload

It's easy to get overwhelmed from the continual barrage of information most people experience these days. What's overwhelming is trying to take in or make meaning out of too many things at once. The overload worsens when you are faced with too many different contexts or multiple interruptions. During information overload, the mind shuts down and you often can't remember what you were thinking a few minutes ago. People over forty like to call these "senior moments," not realizing that many in their twenties are experiencing the same thing. Information overload nearly pushed Amber over the edge:

> *At work, I was asked to keep up with market developments via Internet search engines. At first it was fun. I stayed up half the night hooked on the Net and on caffeine. After a few weeks, I was on overload but didn't stop. I was losing sleep, which affected my ability to focus. I finally went into burnout. I could barely make it through a workday and at night was unable to do much but heat up a prepackaged dinner in the microwave then crawl into bed.*

When the mind assigns too much significance to something, it has to draw energy from your emotional reserves to sustain the importance. The more important something feels, the more energy it draws. If your mind has assigned major importance to several areas at the same time (job issue, relationship issue, financial issue), then the overload can exhaust your emotional and physical energy reserves fast. Using the tools when you are in information overload and telling yourself to take the significance out can help you sort out what is essential and let go of what's not.

Overinvesting Emotional Energy

Have you ever put a ton of energy into a fun project, like planning what you're going to buy or redecorating your house? You think about it a lot, and your desire to get it done adds emotional energy to those thoughts. This can be creative at first. But then when you try to focus on something else, your mind keeps going back to the project and you can't turn it off. Excited emotional energy acts like fuel that keeps the mind going after you take your foot off the pedal. It's hard to be present for other things or focus on anything else. It's the extra emotional investment energy you put into the project that fuels the obsession. You find yourself in overwhelm.

You can stop the runaway momentum and come back to balance using Power of Neutral and the Heart Lock-In technique. Understand that it can take the body a while to wind down and find a new rhythm. As you rest in neutral, you can see that what's going on inside you is a mechanical process, like a computer's hard drive winding down. You slow it down as you hold to neutral and let the runaway mental and emotional energy wind down. You don't have to feel anxious that it's controlling you for long. Use Heart Lock-In then to help smooth out your emotional energy and rebuild your energy reserves.

Stimulation Overload

Many adults and children stay on stimulation overload. They move from stimulation to stimulation: coffee, food, shopping, the Internet, movies, TV, computer games, and so forth. Advertisers keep raising the ante to keep you hooked on stimulation. There are so many things to do and buy. If it's not new or different, it's boring. You get intuitive signals from the heart to chill or slow down. But when you're on the fast track, your mind can disregard what your heart intuition is trying to say.

Heart rhythm coherence will help you recoup your energy between periods of intense stimulation. Use the overwhelm tools to take a break from overinvesting emotional energy or from stimulation overload. Use the Heart Lock-in techniques to rebalance your energies and listen to your heart.

Opening Up a New Room

When you're caught in overwhelm, it's like being in a room that's locked. All you can imagine is more of the same. But shifting to heart rhythm coherence and heart alignment opens up a new room. Debbie, one of the authors of this book, explains how this works:

> *When I get overwhelmed, my mind gets in a box. I can only see what I have to do that can't be done unless I rush, rush, rush. Then I get frustrated if other people interrupt or don't do what I expect. I've learned time and again that rushing or getting frustrated are my signals to use Power of Neutral and Attitude Breathing until I feel detached from my project and to-do list. I use the tools until I can really let it all go for a few minutes. Sometimes I have to sincerely ask myself, "What would I do differently if I were to die tomorrow?" That puts things in perspective fast.*
>
> *Once I find heart alignment, it opens up a new room of possibilities. It's like the clouds clear and the sun comes out. I see from a helicopter level instead of from a freeway rush-hour bottleneck. Shifting to the heart releases a magic. Something pops out of nowhere*

revealing that a task doesn't need to be done or can be put off for some time, or people appear who are able and willing to help. I get a different view of people and see that they are doing the best they can. Priorities get done more easily.

I have experienced this shift into the new room so many times, yet at times I still get pulled back into the overwhelm trap. Then I remember what I did before to find clear air again. It's worth gold to go through it again and keep using these tools to prove this to myself. The tools take you to a place deeper than thinking positive or time management. I tried all that. It finally took plain old letting go and realigning it all from my heart instead of my mind to transform my old feelings of overwhelm. It makes a huge difference.

Activating Your Creative Power

Heart alignment is what unleashes creativity to find nonlinear ways through life's mazes. You operate in a multifunctional way that is effective and in a flow. Remember, creativity isn't found just in art, music, or writing a great report. It's especially about dealing with life challenges that seem to have no solutions.

You can learn to prevent or manage overwhelm before your world tilts out of control. Starting your day with the Heart Lock-In technique and using it before bed, along with practicing the overwhelm tools during the day, will help you keep a balanced perspective. Even in a chaotic society, it's possible for you to manage your emotional energy and stay empowered through heart alignment. The choice is yours.

chapter 8

Getting Relief from Anxiety Disorders

We gain strength, and courage, and confidence by each experience in which we really stop to look fear in the face. . . . We must do that which we think we cannot.

—Eleanor Roosevelt

Underneath a lot of anxiety disorders are resistant or stuck feelings. Sometimes they create pain, a burning sensation, or a feeling of blockage in the area of the heart. The mind's tendency is to "chew" on resistant feelings, trying to figure them out. When the mind can't, it creates angst. Millions today are suffering with this type of angst.

Experts have a name for ongoing anxiety that occurs more days than not over a period of six months. As we mentioned in the introduction, it's called generalized anxiety disorder (GAD), and it's the most common of the anxiety disorders, which include panic, obsessive-compulsive disorder, phobia, and post-traumatic stress disorder. GAD starts with repetitive unmanaged thoughts and emotions that generate anxiety. It soon turns into a physical experience — pain in the heart area, a racing or pounding heart, shortness of breath, muscle tension, fatigue, insomnia, irritability, or an inability to really relax. Having anxiety is nothing to feel bad about. You simply haven't known how to effectively deal with it. But now you *can* — and must — to improve your life.

Getting relief from an anxiety disorder involves taking the angst out of your reactions and treating the underlying, preset pattern.

Presets

Like radio stations that are programmed or preset to come on at the push of a button, your brain has presets that mechanically come on when something triggers them. Sometimes those triggers are your own thoughts or feelings, or a person, place, or issue. Sometimes presets just get activated, and you don't know why. Examples of presets include flashbacks of traumatic experiences, obsessive thoughts or compulsive behaviors, phobia or panic, or thoughts that come up and take control, like "I just know I'm going to panic if I go into that elevator."

Identify your presets and use Cut-Thru worksheets and the Cut-Thru and Heart Lock-In techniques to help soften a rigid pattern and see what's underneath. Gina tells how she used these two techniques to release a preset that had affected her throughout her life:

> *My TMJ (tense jaws) caused me a lot of pain and anxiety. I'd tried many treatments and the dentists kept telling me it was stress. In using Cut-Thru, I became aware of a preset where I told myself that I had to work hard in life to be worthy of love and*

attention. I spent most of the time in steps 5 and 6, dissolving the significance and sincerely asking my heart for help. I followed up the next day with a Heart Lock-In, and during that time I received an intuitive picture of an event from many years earlier.

With wrenching pain I saw someone I loved and admired slipping away from me and forming a close bond with someone else. In my Lock-In, I soaked this picture and this pain in the solvent of my heart and just sent it love.

Gina found that continuing to soak the memory in love began to change her feelings about it.

I found I was coming into a neutral feeling about it and became open to a possibility that maybe what had happened was really just right. What if it was? And what if it wasn't the result of some big misstep on my part?

She began to realize that her pain came from feeling that she should have said or done more to create the closeness she'd wanted with this person. It occurred to her that perhaps, after all, what had happened was really okay in the large scheme of things.

Pondering this possibility, my intuition showed me the origins of this pattern. As a child, I'd adored my father, yet was shy. When I was a young teen, my father suddenly began to devote his attention to my younger brother. I felt shut out. I was hurt and shocked, then became resentful and hardened. I turned to making good grades to get the acknowledgment that I needed.

Soaking these memories in her heart, Gina received another insight.

> *Yes, my brother had gotten the attention, but he'd also gotten the heat. He carries the baggage of that now and its scars, and I carried only a little of it — I had been left alone, but peacefully so. My heart began to melt as I felt a new care and tenderness for my brother, who had been 'on the front lines.' I have a deeper respect for my brother now. I also have new respect for myself and more peace and appreciation for this journey of life I've been on. I feel better.*

Preoccupations

Preoccupations are mental presets that get stuck on "repeat" and lead to emotional brooding and a feeling of heaviness. Performance anxiety; comparing yourself to others; insecurities about what others think of you; fears that you might not get what you want or need usually lie underneath. Preoccupations drain emotional energy like a leaking faucet, and when that's used up they start draining your nerve energy as well. That can lead to neurological misfiring and obsessive-compulsive or addictive behaviors. Addictions give temporary relief from obsessive thoughts and feelings. The real addiction, however, is to the preoccupations themselves.

Preoccupations can start with just one thought followed by a feeling, then another thought, then another feeling — until you are caught in an anxiety or fear loop. You rehearse worst-case scenarios of what might happen — how someone will think of you, talk to you, treat you.

Many people are aware of their anxiety-producing preoccupations and are weary of them. But they may not be *sincerely* tired of them yet — the kind of tired where your heart intelligence makes a statement that you must do something about the problem and you act on it. Even if you haven't reached that point yet, you can break through emotional inertia just by looking at how much energy you lose daily to preoccupations and emotional brooding. If you're honest with yourself, the tally might make you get seriously tired of them quickly.

To get relief, start by *stopping* the emotional investment in preoccupations. To do this, pause now and consider what anxiety preoccupations may be draining your energy. Start with thoughts and feelings that often arise when you wake up in the morning, and then scan through a typical day until you go to bed. See if you can notice any correlation between an anxiety preoccupation about someone or something and physical symptoms or behaviors you typically experience throughout a day or a week. You might also want to try this exercise tomorrow and write your preoccupations down in the journal you're keeping.

Writing down your preoccupations helps get them out of your head and starts to depersonalize them. Using emotion-refocusing tools like Power of Neutral when preoccupations start to take over will help stop the energy drain. Then, using emotional restructuring techniques like Attitude Breathing, Cut-Thru, and Heart Lock-In will create the pattern interrupt you need to transform them.

Surveys show that the tools and techniques described in this book work quickly to help people get release from anxiety. HeartMath training programs conducted in Fortune 50 corporations (including Hewlett-Packard, Cisco Systems, BP, and Unilever), governmental organizations (including NASA and the military), health care systems like Kaiser Permanente, and dozens of schools have achieved very similar results. Culled survey data collected over two years from 1,519 individuals representing a wide variety of organizations and professions indicated that 504 people (33 percent) initially reported feeling anxious "fairly often" to "always." In the follow-up assessments administered one to two months after they were taught the HeartMath tools, 74 percent of these people reported less anxiety, and, on average, their anxiety scores were 40 percent lower.

Scott, a special projects manager in a multinational corporation, used the tools to address his anxiety preoccupation while his division went through downsizing.

> *Anxiety was at an all-time high, and morale at an all-time low. It had been very difficult for me to maintain my perspective and poise because I was angry at the situation. Through consistently practicing Power of Neutral and Attitude Breathing along with telling myself to take the significance out of things, I was able to neutralize my anxiety almost completely, which astonished even me. I found myself going through the workday with a sense of buoyancy and clarity, and able to make decisions with a much greater sense of self-confidence. My coworkers noticed and commented on it. I was much less affected by the chaos and despondency shared by my colleagues.*

How Health Professionals Use HeartMath Tools

Many health professionals use HeartMath tools and techniques to help their patients and themselves. Below are a few examples.

A clinical social worker in private practice spends one day each week at an urban low-cost clinic. His patients suffer from diagnoses ranging from generalized anxiety disorder to complex post-traumatic stress disorder. He says,

> *Therapy often stirs up memories and emotions. I find with the HeartMath tools I can teach my patients how to soothe and ground themselves. They can change their mind about a problem and discover new ways to manage their emotions rather than feeling controlled by them.*

A psychologist wrote,

> *J.L. is in transition in a very difficult way. When I first met her she was exceptionally distressed. However, after just three of her block of ten sessions, she told me the work we are doing has been transformational. I was very moved by her words and acknowledged her for the commitment and time she is putting into her practices. She told me that she spent an hour doing a Cut-Thru on an issue that had been distressing her deeply for thirty-five years, and it has gone away.*

Peter Gruenewald, MD, who specializes in treating emotional and behavioral difficulties, wrote:

> *I am impressed with the speed and depth of efficacy of these tools. A fifty-six-year-old patient had been suffering with non-epileptic fits for about six months, about four a week, with loss of consciousness lasting for about three to five minutes. This gave her extreme anxiety. Since the fits started six months ago, she felt spaced-out and weak and was worried all the time about the reoccurrence of the fits. At her first consultation the patient appeared desperate. She had a hard time finding anything to appreciate, so I taught*

*her the Heart Lock-In technique, focusing on inner
calm, and advised her to practice Power of Neutral
and Attitude Breathing of calm for at least four weeks
before moving on to practice appreciation. She
returned four weeks later and was free of any fits,
saying that she started feeling her old self again. She
has been free of fits for eight weeks now.*

*For myself, I have become aware that there have
been deeper feelings hiding behind an explosive anger I
have at times, like fear of losing control and fear of
rejection. Attitude Breathing and Heart Lock-In have
helped me to manage these fears and their expressions
in the form of anger and frustration, an effect which I
was not able to achieve in my now twenty-five-year-
long regular daily meditative practice.*

Panic Attacks

Many people have used the tools and techniques to stop
panic attacks in their tracks, then reduce their frequency and
even eliminate them. Linda says,

*I have had panic attacks for many years. I felt a fear
of lack of control then fear of an attack coming on,
which is what seemed to bring it on. Now when it
starts to come on, I do Attitude Breathing and breathe
a positive feeling in through my heart and out
through my solar plexus and down into my feet. I
hold steady in the heart and say to myself, "I can
handle this. I know where this is going to go and it's
not worth it. I'm not going there this time." I just
hold to that steady knowingness that I can handle it
by going to my heart, and then it quickly subsides*

*and doesn't go through the whole play-out of fear,
physical attack, and so on.*

Obsessive-Compulsive Behaviors

Sheila had a multitude of anxiety disorders most of her life,
one of them being obsessive-compulsive behaviors. At any
time, a new compulsive behavior could surface.

*I was over forty when I started to compulsively
double-check if a door was locked after I'd locked it.
By default and out of a sense of responsibility, I
became the main person at my company who made
sure all the doors were locked up at night. I began to
catch myself going back one or more times to
double-check that the doors were locked and started to
do that at home as well.*

*I read a self-help book on compulsive behavior,
and one step was to do the behavior consciously and
then walk away and not go back and double-check
yourself. Another step was when the urge to go back
came over you, to engage in a positive activity
instead. I was also using the HeartMath tools, so I
decided to combine the tools with the advice from the
book. I taught myself to be very conscious of what I
was doing when I locked a door. Instead of engaging
in a positive activity, which was not practical when I
was walking away from locking a door, I used
Attitude Breathing, breathing through my heart and
engaging a positive feeling in the heart. I did not
allow myself to go back and check the door. Over time
the anxious feeling of having to double-check the lock
eased away. I also began to trust that most likely I
had locked the door and that everything was alright. I*

no longer have to slowly and consciously lock a door.
I know when I walk away that I have done it.

Sheila had also developed a colon problem with intense pain, inability to process most foods, and severe weight loss. After much testing, the doctors found a parasite in her colon and said it would take some years for her system to normalize, if ever.

After that I developed a fear of germs. Often the fear
would just run in my system as an ongoing anxiety
and as a compulsion to wash my hands over and over.
Even though I tried not washing my hands and
creating a positive attitude, I found I needed to take on
the underlying anxiety and fear around germs in
general. The fear was so strong, I began to apply
Attitude Breathing a positive feeling in though the
heart and out through the solar plexus and bottom of
my feet. I found it best to do this in an animated way
with strong intention. Sometimes I would engage in a
physical exercise while I did the breathing. Over time
and with much diligent practice, the feeling of fear and
anxiety around germs began to fade as did the obsessive
behavior. As my emotions came more into balance
around this and other issues, my colon also healed.

Phobias

Phobias can be incapacitating. A phobia many people have is fear of giving a talk in front of a large group. It can sometimes help to picture a positive audience or look for a friendly face in the crowd. However, it's much more effective to take a few minutes before the talk to shift the feeling of anxiety toward a feeling of deeper care or love for the audience, or compassion and appreciation for yourself giving the talk. Since your discomfort about the situation is fueled by a feeling, it's just more efficient to address the feeling directly.

Often when people try to get over a fear, they focus on the object of the fear, in this case the audience, rather than on the *feeling* of the fear. To transform this type of fear, you have to first clear the insecurity or fear of humiliation or rejection underneath. By learning to shift to a more positive feeling of care and appreciation for the audience or yourself, you perceive the fear in a new light. Positive emotion brings in more coherence and security to clear the fear.

Claustrophobia

Christiane tells her story:

I have always had a fear of being in confined spaces. Journeys in subways that took longer than a few minutes, elevators, and especially tunnels became more and more difficult. I would try to calm myself, but I would become more agitated and my body more cramped. We were in a place where daily we had a drive through a series of long tunnels. I was grabbing the seat, feeling cold and sweaty and breathing shallowly. My husband suggested I should try a HeartMath exercise he showed me.

I started to breathe consciously very slowly through my heart, and after about two minutes I combined this with reliving positive memories, feeling them again. Instantly, it made getting through the closed space more bearable. I practiced this exercise once a day and built up something like a "positivity library" consisting of many different memories: situations with people I love, experiences of nature or

*pieces of art or music that brought me peace and joy.
I also visualized myself going through a tunnel or
being trapped in an elevator and brought up the
negative emotions in myself in order to replace them
with my positive feelings, which became more and
more easily accessible and real. I did this until I was
driving through tunnels in my imagination relaxed
and joyful. I did the same exercise in very short
versions every time I was actually in a closed space.
At the end of the second week of practice, I had not
even registered when we drove through the tunnels,
and my husband made me aware that I had forgotten
to do the exercises. Closed spaces haven't been a
problem since.*

For some, fear is a lifelong experience. Even when fear
has been branded into your neural circuits due to genetic dis-
position or a traumatic shock, with enough coherent heart
power you can take out the emotional imprint and reprogram
those circuits.

Fear of Driving

Christiane provided another transformative story:

*I had never been a keen driver and had always been
apprehensive about driving in cities. A very bad
accident very close to our home, resulting in two
deaths and severe injuries of friends and colleagues,
aggravated my fears into a phobia about driving. I'd
break out in cold sweats and my heart would race
when I drove. I spent ages making unnecessary turns
because I was too scared to change lanes. Finally I
gave up driving.*

After a few months of practicing HeartMath tools on my fear of closed spaces, I gained enough confidence to apply them to driving. I was getting quite good at cutting through negative emotions or experiences by shifting to positive feelings and connecting with my intuition. I did not need to imagine positive situations anymore, but could straight away access the feeling of tranquility whenever I became conscious that I needed it. So I was ready to tackle driving.

First, I imagined all sorts of driving situations and journeys. I tried to allow my fears to come up and live through them, in order to use Power of Neutral and Attitude Breathing to transform them into a positive feeling. It worked. I started driving again. Then my husband bought me a car. Now it was for real. I did slow Attitude Breathing when getting in the car and reminded myself of the positive feeling during my exercises. After a short time, I realized that the fears were gone and for the first time in my driving life I actually enjoyed it. After about two months, I even started driving my husband's sports car and I really enjoy that. Now, whenever I do slow Attitude Breathing and let positivity flow in, panic and fear are completely gone.

You have to "negotiate" anxieties and phobias out of your system through dialogue between your mind and heart. The practices Christiane did and the Cut-Thru and Heart Lock-In techniques serve as important negotiators. You can start your practice of these techniques by asking your heart to give you an animated review of anxieties you have about yourself, people, and situations. Then ask your heart intelligence to show you a better way to deal with each one. It will, in a creative way, as you proceed through the steps. If you feel stuck, be heart vulnerable and talk to a friend or counselor.

Keep a journal and write down what your heart intelligence says to do. Have patience as you act on what your heart says. Don't beat yourself up if anxiety comes back or you're afraid to do what your heart says. Take it one step at a time, but keep moving forward.

Dread

One of the last things to go before you can completely release anxiety and fear, and one of the hardest to let go of, is dread. After you've stored enough significance in anxiety or fear, it can cause a sensation of dread. You color what might happen in the next moment or later with a gloomy sense of apprehension. Whether it's about communications with someone, home or work issues, or clearing out the blackberry bushes behind the house, there are always plenty of things ahead you could dread.

You can almost feel the iron knot of dread in the pit of your stomach as you drag yourself toward something that feels bigger than you or you stall to avoid it. "Oh, I've really tried"; "It's hard"; "It doesn't seem to work, but I'll keep trying"; "Well, I know I better go for it, because if I don't, things will just get worse." These are the typical results of meek attempts to overcome dread.

A more constructive way to deal with a dread is to approach it as an *attitude* you need to change. Take a moment to focus in the heart, and make your most sincere effort to replace a feeling of dread with excitement. This may sound radical, but even if you get only halfway there, you've freed up a lot of energy. If you get all the way there, you've discovered an empowering freedom and continuous resource of energy. Or try this: In the midst of your reluctance, do something caring that benefits yourself or others. Shifting to an attitude or feeling of care even for a few minutes brings in renewed energy and can also shift your perception about the issue you were dreading.

> *Aimee lived with a sense of dread much of the time. "It's not that I'm great at dealing with challenges. But for some reason, I seem to attract them. When a difficult challenge arises, I immediately feel fear, self-doubt, and dread! This makes me so tired I barely have enough energy to face the project and then haul myself through it," she lamented.*
>
> *Recently Aimee faced one of those challenging situations. "But this time, as the automatic feeling of dread started, I decided to use the situation as an opportunity for growth, and try heart soaking. I took the time to find a feeling of soft heart and soak there, which immediately relaxed the knot in my stomach. I then focused on appreciating the chance to change, asking my heart to help me transform dread into opportunity." Aimee was amazed by her body's response. "A subtle excitement flooded my system, and the dread melted away. This made me realize that with some practice I could get rid of my long relationship with dread and just move on through whatever challenges life brings. It was a hopeful moment."*

Sometimes the sense of dread can be overpowering, especially if you anticipate a big and uncertain change in your future. Stella, who had been practicing the tools, tells us how she handled the dread when Darian, her fiancé, was suddenly diagnosed with an incurable illness:

Somehow, being in a situation like this makes you really appreciate how the heart can save you a lot of pain and confusion. I had to deal with the dread. Every time a thought would come up that had an emotional charge of fear or anxiety, I would anchor back to the heart with Attitude Breathing. I focused on taking the significance out of the situation as best I could and was able to get calm.

Stella found that practicing the tools throughout the process of receiving the diagnosis and getting educated about the illness kept her emotions in balance, which helped her make needed decisions more rationally.

I felt like I gave Darian great support and was doing the best I could do for him by staying steady in the heart, poised for anything. I knew it would be harder for him if he had to deal with my anxiety and dread on top of his own response.

As the months progressed, Stella realized that one of the biggest energy drains when caring for a person with an incurable illness is overcare and a sense of guilt that you can't do anything to help.

Staying in the heart and taking out the significance helped me live in the now and made it so much easier to get used to this illness in our lives.

Darian talked about his own experience:

I've always been inclined to be the one who takes care of others, and sometimes this got me into meddling, trying to fix other people's situations for them. Well, eight months ago I got a wake-up call that forced me to find balance with all that when I was diagnosed with multiple sclerosis.

As the doctor delivered the news, Darian found all his worst fears coming up: "How will I take care of my family? How will I keep my job? How will I stay active? What will people think of me?" He dreaded going home from the hospital. "My projections of what would happen ran rampant. I was scared."

Driving home from the hospital, Darian practiced the Cut-Thru technique.

> *It was only after breathing through the heart in step 2 that I remembered that the doctor said that getting MS at my age (forty-seven) could possibly be not as bad as if I'd gotten it earlier in life. As I assumed objectivity about the situation in step 3, I realized I could be in a lot worse shape. When I applied step 4, rest in neutral, I realized I was overreacting, and my mature heart told me, "There's no cure, so just do the best you can." I then took my situation and soaked my feelings about it. For the first time I could feel sincere compassion for myself without feeling sorry for myself.*

Darian's dread started to dissolve.

> *As I took the significance out, an insight came to me: If I took care of myself more, I'd be able to take care of others better and my sincerity would increase. I could keep growing and have meaningful relationships. Over the months since then, I sense that the overcaring and meddling I used to do has been transforming into deeper and more sincere connections with people. I value the moments that we have together, rather than trying to fix them for the future.*

Learning to Live in the Now

Valuing the moments, or living in the now, is about having more of your *real self* show up in each moment. Becoming more of who you really are brings satisfaction, and effectiveness at being yourself is what brings you fulfillment.

Since most anxieties, fears, or dreads are predicated on what happened in the past or on projections about the future, gathering your energies to be fully present in the now—which is the only time you have control over—gives you power. It's in this moment, now, and the next moment, *now*, that you have the power to be the architect of yourself. Remember that anxiety disorders are not *you*; they are presets, preoccupations, and familiar neural patterns. You can create a pattern interrupt and create your way out. Step-by-step you can create a future free of anxiety and full of renewed vitality as you develop the ability to feel better in the now.

chapter 9

Building Resilience

The heart is the perfection of the whole organism. Therefore the principles of the power of perception and the soul's ability to nourish itself must lie in the heart.

— Aristotle

It's obvious, given the increasing stress levels in society, why anxiety is a problem for more and more people. It just makes practical common sense to build your own capacity to navigate through it all by using the potential within your own heart. It's your heart that gives you the intelligence and power to flex through challenging situations with less stress and downtime. And it's your heart that gives you the resilience to bounce back faster when you get down. We call it *heart buoyancy*. Like a buoy in the water, you may bob up and down, but you stay afloat.

Heart Buoyancy

Dr. Anne Berlin, a psychologist, says,

> *Many of the women I see in my practice are deep in
> overcare. By the time they get to me, they feel
> drained. Some are having panic attacks or anxiety,
> waking up in the middle of the night, overcaring
> about something that they didn't resolve during the
> day. These women need help before they break down
> with an anxiety disorder or depression. I've been
> using HeartMath tools with many of my patients. I
> find that 40 percent experience some immediate relief
> in the first session. If they continue to practice,
> another 30 percent begin experiencing relief within
> four sessions. They're able to calm themselves down,
> regulate their heart rhythms, increase their energy,
> and they love it because they feel more in control.*

Coherence tools, like Attitude Breathing, can release
wonderful feelings that get distributed throughout your system, generating heart buoyancy. Heart buoyancy doesn't
mean jumping up and down with joy. It's a lightness and
strength that lets you know that you are in control of yourself. You learn to see how much of your anxiety has been due
to a lack of resilience that would allow you to flex and make
attitude adjustments as you go.

More people are feeling the sense of time speeding up
and dragging them with it. So don't feel like it's all just happening to you. Stress, overwhelm, and anxiety will continue
to increase across the world because people don't know what
to do to stop it. You have to finally activate your own power
to create your way out of stress and overwhelm. Without
enough heart buoyancy, stress and overwhelm will take you
under. With the coherence tools, you can recover quickly

instead of going through so much downtime. Heart buoyancy helps you stay balanced while you're waiting for something to help bail out a situation or at least make it better. It also helps magnetize facilitation in ways you wouldn't expect.

Tips to Reduce Social Anxiety

Stop projecting into the future. Ask your heart intelligence to help you become more aware when you are mechanically making negative projections about the future—about other people, situations, or issues. You can stop a lot of projections, even if you can't stop them all. Use the tool Notice and Ease, and remember that negative projections become anxiety generators. Take the significance out of fear projections, even if only a little, and you'll release a lot of anxiety. Try reminding yourself there's enough mounting anxiety in the world without you contributing to its formidable momentum.

Make an inner agreement with yourself to deal with life's situations day to day and moment to moment. Even as you make that pact with yourself, some part of you will stop projecting and relax, which will help take out more significance and anxiety. Have patience. You may not stop all worry or anxiety, but with each increment of progress, the energy saved will accumulate and staying in the moment will get easier.

When you can't stop worrying, use the Power of Neutral tool. The mind believes things are the way it perceives them. After all, it's right a lot of the time, and so it must be right this time. Instead of spending your emotional resources worrying, try holding to neutral so you can see from a more sober, objective view. Once that's done, you are more likely to find a solution to suit the need. Holding to neutral creates a space for more possibilities to emerge from your heart intelligence. Neutral is a place to go where emotional maturity grows. Use Attitude Breathing to help release the worry pattern. If worry keeps returning, breathe in through the heart and out through the solar plexus and down through the feet to release the mind and emotions and anchor your energy.

Use Power of Neutral when you overpersonalize what someone says. The neutral tool helps to slow down your emotional reactions. What if the other person didn't really mean it as personally as you heard it? If that's the case, see if you can find humor in your reactions and learn to laugh at yourself more. It's obvious that some comments will be hard to neutralize. Still, using the neutral tool can help you find a more heart-intelligent response. Perhaps you need to be heart vulnerable and sincere with that person or with a friend to clear your feelings and regain balance.

When other people's anxiety or negativity gets to you. Try using the key words of the Heart Lock-In technique steps, "Shift, Activate, Send," when your emotions are getting pulled by other people's anxiety or negativity. *Shift* your attention away from your mind and emotions and focus in your heart *Activate,* and *Send* a positive feeling of love, care, appreciation, or compassion to your environment and to yourself. You can "Shift, Activate, Send" while listening or talking, reading or watching the news. This will help buffer you from others' negativity and can at times help those around you find more balance.

Activate more real care. Care acts as a tonic for your nervous system. When negativity surrounds you, ask yourself, "What would be the most caring attitude I could have right now?" Take on that attitude and breathe that attitude through the heart. Then ask yourself, "What would be the most caring action I could take right now?" Do it. Breathe the attitude of care as you act on that. Just assuming an attitude of real care (not overcare) will start to create an emotional shift. Hold the attitude and allow any overcare or anxiety to move out of your system. If you find a pleasant feeling, hold onto it and send that feeling to all the cells in your body to help anchor it in. You'll be surprised at how much relief and renewed energy that real care can bring to you. As you increase your care for others as well as for yourself, you keep emotional clutter from accumulating.

When you feel awkward. It will eventually start to feel awkward to linger in overcare, overwhelm, and anxiety. You feel awkward because you now know too much. It's like being stuck between two radio stations, one broadcasting the old anxiety, and the other your new insights. You see how the old anxiety saps you, but you may not yet be able to immediately follow your new insights. When this happens, keep using the tools, and keep taking steps to put insight into action. Learn to make peace with what isn't yet peaceful, without judging yourself or the process as good or bad, right or wrong. The distance between you and your goal shortens as you appreciate every step of progress along the way. Appreciate having tools that can help you.

Developing Business Heart

Practicing the tools develops what we call *business heart*. It's an aspect of heart intelligence that "means business." Remember that *you* are accountable for your emotions and energy. With business heart, you notice anxious feelings, then you *do* something to transform them. You set firm limits on old reactions you keep on allowing and caving into, even though you know better. You mean business using the tools and stay focused on each step, instead of multitasking other things in your mind as you practice. When anxiety sucks you in, business heart says, "I can't afford this," then uses Power of Neutral and Attitude Breathing to stop the drain. Keep telling yourself, "I don't need this anymore. I absolutely cannot afford it." You can't afford to do it anymore because you don't want to have to pick up the pieces every time. Each time you just say no and follow through, you build more resilience to flex through challenges. You don't have to feel bad if the anxiety doesn't completely go away. Just realize that overwhelm and anxiety are not you – *not your real self.* You can learn to smile at yourself and say, "I'm not going there."

Monitoring Your Heart Rhythms

Learning to shift into heart rhythm coherence and sustain it for longer periods of time builds heart buoyancy and power. You can get scientific about your practice and monitor your coherence levels by using a software and hardware system called HeartMath's Freeze-Framer Interactive Learning System, a heart rhythm coherence monitor and pulse sensor. You can watch your heart rhythms on your computer screen change from incoherent to coherent in real time as you use the tools. The Freeze-Framer, developed by Doc, helps you build your coherence skills through four challenge levels and fun software games. You use the games to reinforce your tool practices. Being able to see even a little improvement in sustaining coherence is a real confidence booster.

A psychologist who uses the Freeze-Framer in his practice wrote,

> Brent, a forty-five-year-old male, had an anxiety disorder and problems with anger. After fifteen sessions he successfully achieved a medium level of coherence on the monitor. This provided confidence to Brent, and he began to use the tools during the day

*when feelings of anxiety or anger arose. He accepted
the suggestion to practice twice daily when he had no
anger or anxiety in order to build and sustain
coherence. At his last visit, Brent achieved a 30
percent level of high coherence. Several months later,
he wrote a note expressing how calm and peaceful his
life had become.*

Karen was seeing a doctor for help with irritable bowel syndrome. She had a long-standing history of anxiety, panic disorder, and depression that isolated her from family and society, so the doctor introduced her to the Freeze-Framer. He describes her progress:

*By her fourth session she had made significant gains
in her level of coherence. During that session Karen
became tearful then sobbed uncontrollably, admitting
to me that she was overmedicating herself and had
suicidal ideations. She acknowledged to me that her
life did have meaning and that achieving this level of
coherence was so cathartic for her. As she continued
her coherence practice, the anxiety and physical
symptoms diminished. Karen began to slowly reengage
with her family, care for her children, and integrate
back into society.*

A psychologist at Brooks Air Force Base in Texas uses the Freeze-Framer to treat soldiers returning from Iraq with post-traumatic stress disorder (PTSD).

*I'm using the Freeze-Framer as an adjunct treatment
modality in a primary care clinic and have found it
an effective tool for many conditions that returning
soldiers are suffering from, including anxiety states,
PTSD, depression, and physical pain. Military
members with social anxiety are also finding help.*

Cadets with test anxiety have seen improved scores. I hope to use the Freeze-Framer with the basic trainees as a method of helping with the stress of basic training. This is a mobile tool that can be used easily with medical military operations in the field.

Renewing Your Intent

The coherence tools and techniques work, but of course you are the one who makes them work. It's important not to look at the tools as quick fixes, as if they are magic, because that can lead to idealistic expectations. If you overexpect from a tool, you are likely to forget the part that *you* have to play to make it work. Periodically, review the steps of the tools and techniques as if you're learning them for the first time, so they don't become just conceptual to you. Practice regularly, and practice genuinely and from the heart. Occasionally review your journal or notebook and the paragraphs in this book that especially apply to you. In this way, you will be able to get the most out of the techniques, as well as keep track of your progress. The tools and exercises you've learned in this book bring new refinement to your thoughts and feelings as you deepen your heart alignment. Renewing your intent each time you practice will give you the most mileage.

When you think the tools and techniques aren't working for you, usually what's missing is sustaining your intent, especially when your feelings won't shift right away. Renew your intent to admit and befriend those feelings. Then be neutral about *whatever* you are feeling. Breathe an attitude replacement through your heart, and allow incoherent or troubling feelings some time to clear, without identifying with them and storing significance again. Often, being heart vulnerable and talking with a friend can bring release or show you your next step.

Don't forget to use the Cut-Thru technique when troubled feelings and thoughts still won't release. Make an integrity pact with yourself to assign troubled feelings to soak in the heart and not invest more mental energy in them. Try visualizing the compassion of your heart as liquid gold, and heart soaking as alchemy that transforms stuck feelings. (Gold represents powerful liquid love, like rays of warmth from sunshine.) Try to breathe gold through your heart while soaking until you feel better. Be gentle with yourself. Befriend the process of clearing. Don't let performance anxiety about doing it right or how long it's taking sap your energy.

Heart soaking can bring some pleasant surprises. You see old things with new eyes. What if a fear about someone that you have carried around for years can be replaced by a more current feeling that this person has truly changed? Or that it no longer makes you anxious if they haven't changed?

You Can Do It

The main thing to remember is, even if it takes a little practice, *you do have the power in you to make this work.* Don't give up, even when you have a setback. Everybody has them. They are just curves in the road, not the end of the road. Many challenges are not about what to do—they are about taking the time to go to your heart and then doing what you know. Keep remembering to have compassion for yourself along the way.

The more you open up your heart awareness, the more you'll find your balance in stressful situations. You'll build heart buoyancy to move through them without much energy loss. Learn to listen to your heart and follow your heart. A step at a time, you'll be able to transform overcare and anxiety into free energy and resilience to create the life you really want.

As people transform overwhelm and anxiety at the individual level, it helps encourage and facilitate the collective whole. Look at stress as a challenge to strengthen the power of the heart, not as a predator on the prowl. Through the heart, stress and anxiety can be intelligently transformed. Let's roll up our sleeves and make a difference together.

Tool and Technique Summary

Emotion Admittance

Use the Notice and Ease tool on p. 50 for admitting and easing emotions. Admit what you are feeling, whatever it is—worry, anxiety, frustration, anger, hurt, resistance, numbness, or even a vague disturbance you can't put your finger on. Being honest about naming what you are feeling helps you slow down the emotional energy running through your system and gives you more power.

Emotion Refocusing

Use the Power of Neutral tool on p. 51 to refocus your emotions. Power of Neutral harnesses the rhythmic power of your heart to bring your mind, emotions, and physiology to a state of neutral that can lessen or stop many anxiety triggers. Think of Neutral as a "time-out zone" where you can step back, neutralize your emotions, and see more options with clarity. Use the Power of Neutral when you feel overcare, overidentity, overattachment, perfectionism, or performance anxiety. Use Power of Neutral during difficult communications or when you overpersonalize what someone says.

Emotion Restructuring

Use the Attitude Breathing tool on p. 57 to help you shift out of a negative emotional state into a positive one (psychologically and physiologically) and gain a more intelligent perspective. As you use Attitude Breathing and breathe a replacement attitude, you restructure your neural patterning and create a new baseline of emotional coherence. Use Attitude Breathing to clear hurt and anger and to stop obsessing, worrying, and negatively projecting. Use Attitude Breathing when you have insecurity projections or anxiety about what you should do or should have done.

Use the emotion restructuring technique Cut-Thru on p. 67 for clearing accumulated and long-standing anxieties and deeper emotional issues. Use the Cut-Thru worksheet on p. 80 to record your insights and keep track of your progress. Memorize the Quick Cut-Thru Steps on p. 81 and use them during the day as needed to build emotional strength and flexibility.

Use the emotion restructuring technique Heart Lock-In on p. 105 to learn how to sustain coherence for longer periods and to establish new neural patterns. Using the Heart Lock-In technique a couple times a day helps to accumulate energy, recharge your emotional system, and cushion the impact of day-to-day stress or anxiety.

Releasing Overwhelm, Project Identity, or Overstimulation

As soon as you feel the strain of too many things hitting at once, use the Power of Neutral tool (p. 51) to step back and reduce the emotional charge. Then to increase heart rhythm coherence, breathe ease and calm while telling yourself to take the significance out of whatever is going on. Let it all go while you're doing the Attitude Breathing (p. 57). Using these overwhelm tools only takes a few minutes, but you have to really *do* it, not try halfway while your mind is thinking about what you haven't gotten done yet. Keep breathing the attitude of ease and calm or breathe balance as you move through your activities to prevent overwhelm from recurring.

Healing Hurt and Pain

Use Notice and Ease, and be heart vulnerable with yourself (p. 50). Use Power of Neutral (p. 51) and Attitude Breathing (p. 57) to bring in more coherence. Listen to your heart for insight and direction. When you can't clear the hurt or pain in the moment or the emotional history keeps resurfacing, use the Cut-Thru technique with a Cut-Thru worksheet (p. 80). Befriend the process of healing. If blame and sadness take over, realize it's just the stored feelings spinning out of your system. It doesn't mean that you're not making progress. Hold to neutral about *whatever* you are feeling. It helps to remember that these old feelings are not the real you. Soak them in the heart, and take the significance out as you allow the old feelings to spin out of your system.

Releasing Dread

Approach dread as an *attitude* you need to change. Take a moment to focus in the heart, and make your most sincere effort to replace a feeling of dread with excitement. This may sound radical, but even if you get only halfway there, you've freed up a lot of energy. If you get all the way there, you've discovered an empowering freedom and continuous resource of energy. Shifting to an attitude or feeling of care even for a few minutes brings in renewed energy and can also shift your perception about the issue you were dreading.

Keep Asking Your Heart for Guidance

The heart's intuitive signal is often weaker than the mind at first, so you have to listen carefully and sincerely. The mind sometimes tries to jump in and mask the voice of the heart with "yeah, but," especially when the answer isn't something the mind wants to hear. Heart intuition can also work the other way and be loud and clear. Respect both ways, and realize that the process of learning to listen to the heart takes refinement.

Learn More About HeartMath Products

Explore other HeartMath books, e-books, learning programs, music, software, seminars and professional training to reinforce and advance what you've learned in this book.. More details can be found online at: http://heartmath.com/store/index.html

Books and Learning Programs by Doc Childre

Childre, Doc, and Deborah Rozman. 2003. *Transforming Anger: The HeartMath Solution for Letting Go of Rage, Frustration, and Irritation.* Oakland, Calif.: New Harbinger Publications.

Childre, Doc, and Deborah Rozman. 2005. *Transforming Stress: The HeartMath Solution for Relieving Worry, Fatigue, and Tension* . Oakland, Calif.: New Harbinger Publications.

Childre, Doc, and Howard Martin. 1999. *The HeartMath Solution.* San Francisco: HarperSanFrancisco.

Childre, Doc, and Bruce Cryer. 2000. *From Chaos to Coherence: The Power to Change Performance.* Boulder Creek, Calif.: Planetary Publications.

Childre, Doc. 1996. *Teaching Children to Love: 80 Games and Fun Activities for Raising Balanced Children in Unbalanced Times.* Boulder Creek, Calif.: Planetary Publications.

Childre, Doc. 1992. *The How to Book of Teen Self Discovery.* Boulder Creek, Calif.: Planetary Publications.

From Chaos to Coherence (CD-ROM). HeartMath LLC: Boulder Creek, Calif. and Knowledgebuilder.com.

Music by Doc Childre

Scientifically designed to enhance the practice of HeartMath techniques and tools.

Heart Zones. 1991. Planetary Publications.

Speed of Balance. 1996. Planetary Publications.

Quiet Joy. 2001. Planetary Publications.

Freeze-Framer Software

The Freeze-Framer interactive learning system with patented heart rhythm monitor and three software games allows you to observe your heart rhythms in real-time and assists you in shifting into coherence and sustaining coherence (the Zone of high performance). It is also available in portable, handheld version called emWave Personal Stress Reliever.

HeartMath Seminars and Training

HeartMath provides world class training programs for organizations, hospitals, health care providers and individuals. HeartMath training is available through on-site programs, licensing and certification for organizations, and sponsored workshops, seminars and conference presentations.

Licensing and Certification: Training to Become a One-on-One Provider

HeartMath offers licensing and certification to health care providers, coaches and consultants wanting to use HeartMath tools and technology as part of the services they provide to clients in a one on one professional model.

Telecourses and Coaching

Learn the HeartMath System of tools and techniques from the comfort of your own home or office. Our comprehensive and in-depth Tele-Courses offer personalized instruction on how to enhance your overall sense of well-being, reduce stress and improve performance. Each course includes instruction of a wide range of HeartMath tools, techniques and concepts along with individualize coaching on how to apply them directly in your life.

For information on products, training, and coaching programs, call (800) 450-9111, e-mail info@heartmath.com, visit the Web site at www.heartmath.com, or write to HeartMath, 14700 West Park Avenue, Boulder Creek, CA 95006.

Research and Education

The Institute of HeartMath (IHM) is a nonprofit research and education organization dedicated to understanding emotions and the role of the heart in learning, performance, and well-being. IHM offers two programs for use in educational and classroom settings:

TestEdge programs for improving academic performance and test scores

Teacher Resiliency programs for teachers, administrators, and principals

---

For information about Institute of HeartMath research initiatives and education programs, call (831) 338-8500, e-mail info@ heartmath.org, visit the Web site at www.heartmath.org, or write to Institute of HeartMath, 14700 West Park Avenue, Boulder Creek, CA 95006.

References

Armour, J. A. 2003. *Neurocardiology – Anatomical and functional principles*. Boulder Creek, Calif.: HeartMath Research Center, Institute of HeartMath, Publication No. 03-011.

Armour, J. A., and G. C. Kember. 2004. Cardiac sensory neurons. In *Basic and Clinical Neurocardiology*, edited by J. A. Armour and J. L. Ardell, 79–117. New York: Oxford University Press.

Beidel, D. C., and S. M. Turner. 1997. At risk for anxiety: I. Psychopathology in the offspring of anxious parents. *Journal of the American Academy of Child and Adolescent Psychiatry* 36(7):918–24.

Blakeslee, T. R. 1997. *The Attitude Factor: Extend Your Life by Changing the Way You Think*. London: Thorsons/HarperCollins.

Cameron, O. G. 2002. *Visceral Sensory Neuroscience: Interoception*. New York: Oxford University Press.

Cantin, M., and J. Genest. 1986. The heart as an endocrine gland. *Scientific American* 254(2):76–81.

Danner, D. D., D. A. Snowdon, and W. V. Friesen. 2001. Positive emotions in early life and longevity: Findings from the nun study. *Journal of Personality and Social Psychology* 80(5):804–13.

Epel, E. S., E. H. Blackburn, J. Lin, F. S. Dhabhar, N. E. Adler, J. D. Morrow, and R. M. Cawthon. 2004. Accelerated telomere shortening in response to life stress. *Proceedings of the National Academy of Sciences USA* 101(49):17312-5.

Fredrickson, B. L. 2000. Cultivating positive emotions to optimize health and well-being. *Prevention & Treatment 3:* Article 0001a. http://journals.apa.org/prevention/volume3/pre0030 001a.html.

Fredrickson, B. L. 2002. Positive emotions. In *Handbook of Positive Psychology*, edited by C. R. Snyder and S. J. Lopez, 120-34. New York: Oxford University Press.

Frysinger, R. C., and R. M. Harper. 1990. Cardiac and respiratory correlations with unit discharge in epileptic human temporal lobe. *Epilepsia* 31(2):162-71.

Gershon, M. 1999. *The Second Brain.* San Francisco: HarperCollins.

Goleman, D. 1995. Brain may tag all perceptions with a value. *New York Times*, August 8.

Gutkowska, J., M. Jankowski, S. Mukaddam-Daher, and S. M. McCann. 2000. Oxytocin is a cardiovascular hormone. *Brazilian Journal of Medical and Biological Research* 33:625-33.

Guyton, A. C. 1991. *Textbook of Medical Physiology.* Philadelphia: W. B. Saunders Company.

Isen, A. M. 1987. Positive affect, cognitive processes, and social behavior. In *Advances in Experimental Social Psychology*, Vol. 20, edited by L. Berkowitz, 203-53. New York: Academic Press.

Isen, A. M. 1998. On the relationship between affect and creative problem solving. In *Affect, Creative Experience, and Psychological Adjustment*, edited by S. W. Russ, 3-17. Philadelphia: Brunner/Mazel.

Isen, A. M. 1999. Positive affect. In *Handbook of Cognition and Emotion*, edited by T. Dalgleish and M. Power, 522–39. New York: John Wiley & Sons.

LeDoux, J. 1996. *The Emotional Brain: The Mysterious Underpinnings of Emotional Life*. New York: Simon and Schuster.

Lessmeier, T. J., D. Gamperling, V. Johnson-Liddon, B. S. Fromm, R. T. Steinman, M. D. Meissner, and M. H. Lehmann. 1997. Unrecognized paroxysmal supraventricular tachycardia: Potential for misdiagnosis as panic disorder. *Archives of Internal Medicine* 157:537–43.

McCraty, R. 2003. *Heart–brain neurodynamics: The making of emotions*. Boulder Creek, Calif.: HeartMath Research Center, Institute of HeartMath, Publication No. 03-015.

McCraty, R. 2004. The energetic heart: Bioelectromagnetic communication within and between people. In *Bioelectromagnetic Medicine*, edited by P. J. Rosch and M. S. Markov, 541–62. New York: Marcel Dekker.

McCraty, R. 2006. Emotional stress, positive emotions, and psychophysiological coherence. In *Stress in Health and Disease*, edited by B. B. Arnetz and R. Ekman, 360–385. Weinheim, Germany: Wiley-VCH.

McCraty, R., M. Atkinson, and R. T. Bradley. 2004. Electrophysiological evidence of intuition: Part 2. A system-wide process? *Journal of Alternative and Complementary Medicine* 10(2):325–36.

McCraty, R., M. Atkinson, G. Rein, and A. D. Watkins. 1996. Music enhances the effect of positive emotional states on salivary IgA. *Stress Medicine* 12(3):167–75.

McCraty, R., M. Atkinson, W. A. Tiller, G. Rein, and A. D. Watkins. 1995. The effects of emotions on short-term power spectrum analysis of heart rate variability. *American Journal of Cardiology* 76(14):1089–93.

McCraty, R., M. Atkinson, and D. Tomasino. 2001. *Science of the Heart: Exploring the Role of the Heart in Human Performance*. Boulder Creek, Calif.: HeartMath Research Center; Institute of HeartMath, Publication No. 01-001.

McCraty, R., M. Atkinson, D. Tomasino, and R. T. Bradley. 2005. *The coherent heart: Heart–brain interactions, psychophysiological coherence, and the emergence of system-wide order*. Boulder Creek, Calif.: HeartMath Research Center, Institute of HeartMath, Publication No. 05-022.

McCraty, R., B. Barrios-Choplin, M. Atkinson, and D. Tomasino. 1998. The effects of different music on mood, tension, and mental clarity. *Alternative Therapies in Health and Medicine* 4(1):75–84.

McCraty, R., B. Barrios-Choplin, D. Rozman, M. Atkinson, and A. D. Watkins. 1998. The impact of a new emotional self-management program on stress, emotions, heart rate variability, DHEA and cortisol. *Integrative Physiological and Behavioral Science* 33(2):151–70.

McCraty, R., and D. Childre. 2004. The grateful heart: The psychophysiology of appreciation. In *The Psychology of Gratitude*, edited by R. A. Emmons and M. E. McCullough, 230–55. New York: Oxford University Press.

Phillimore, J. 2001. Terror vision. *The Observer* (London), October 14.

Pribram, K. H., and F. T. Melges. 1969. Psychophysiological basis of emotion. In *Handbook of Clinical Neurology*, Vol. 3, edited by P. J. Vinken and G. W. Bruyn, 316–41. Amsterdam: North-Holland Publishing Company.

Rilke, R. M. 1993. *Letters to a Young Poet*. Translated by M. D. Herter Norton. New York: W. W. Norton.

Sandman, C. A., B. B. Walker, and C. Berka. 1982. Influence of afferent cardiovascular feedback on behavior and the cortical evoked potential. In *Perspectives in Cardiovascular*

Psychophysiology, edited by J. T. Cacioppo and R. E. Petty, 189–222. New York: The Guilford Press.

Sapolsky, R. M. 1992. *Stress, the Aging Brain and the Mechanisms of Neuron Death.* Cambridge, Mass.: MIT Press.

Shealy, N. 1995. A review of dehydroepiandrosterone (DHEA). *Integrative Physiological and Behavioral Science* 30(4):308–13.

Snyder, C. R., and S. J. Lopez, eds. 2002. *Handbook of Positive Psychology.* New York: Oxford University Press.

Tiller, W. A., R. McCraty, and M. Atkinson. 1996. Cardiac coherence: A new, noninvasive measure of autonomic nervous system order. *Alternative Therapies in Health and Medicine* 2(1):52–65.

Doc Childre is the founder and chairman of the scientific advisory board of the Institute of HeartMath, the chairman of HeartMath, LLC, and the chairman and co-CEO of Quantum Intech. He is the author of eight books and a consultant to business leaders, scientists, educators, and the entertainment industry on Intui-Technology®. His HeartMath System and proprietary heart rhythm technology for coherence building, called the **Freeze-Framer,** have been reported on by Newsweek.com, **USA Today,** NBC-**Today Show,** ABC-**Good Morning America,** ABC **World News Tonight, CNN Headline News,** CNN.com, CNN Lou Dobbs, Wall Street Journal, **Harvard Business Review, The Economist's Intelligent Life, Business 2.0, Modern Health Care, Health Leaders, Prevention, Self, Natural Health, Alternative Medicine, Psychology Today, PGA.com, Golf magazine, Golf Illustrated, Allure, Cosmopolitan, FIRST for Women, Woman's World, New Woman, GQ Magazine, Men's Health, Men's Fitness, Los Angeles Times, San Francisco Chronicle, San Jose Mercury News,** and numerous other publications around the world.

Deborah Rozman, Ph.D., is a psychologist with thirty years of experience as a business executive, educator and author. She is President and co-CEO of Quantum Intech, overseeing strategic alliances and the expansion of HeartMath technologies worldwide. Quantum Intech develops and licenses health technologies and products powered by HeartMath that transform anxiety and improve health and performance. Deborah also serves on the Institute of HeartMath's scientific advisory board and Physics of Humanity council. She is a key spokesperson for the HeartMath system, giving media interviews and keynote addresses for executives, scientists, and health and technology companies throughout the world. She is listed in *Who's Who in California.*

Some Other New Harbinger Titles

The End of-life Handbook, Item 5112 $15.95

The Mindfulness and Acceptance Workbook for Anxiety, Item 4993 $21.95

A Cancer Patient's Guide to Overcoming Depression and Anxiety, Item 5044 $19.95

Handbook of Clinical Psychopharmacology for Therapists, 5th edition, Item 5358 $55.95

Disarming the Narcissist, Item 5198 $14.95

The ABCs of Human Behavior, Item 5389 $49.95

Rage, Item 4627 $14.95

10 Simple Solutions to Chronic Pain, Item 4825 $12.95

The Estrogen-Depression Connection, Item 4832 $16.95

Helping Your Socially Vulnerable Child, Item 4580 $15.95

Life Planning for Adults with Developmental Disabilities, Item 4511 $19.95

Overcoming Fear of Heights, Item 4566 $14.95

Acceptance & Commitment Therapy for the Treatment of Post-Traumatic Stress Disorder & Trauma-Related Problems, Item 4726 $58.95

But I Didn't Mean That!, Item 4887 $14.95

Calming Your Anxious Mind, 2nd edition, Item 4870 $14.95

10 Simple Solutions for Building Self-Esteem, Item 4955 $12.95

The Dialectical Behavior Therapy Skills Workbook, Item 5136 $21.95

The Family Intervention Guide to Mental Illness, Item 5068 $17.95

Finding Life Beyond Trauma, Item 4979 $19.95

Five Good Minutes at Work, Item 4900 $14.95

It's So Hard to Love You, Item 4962 $14.95

Energy Tapping for Trauma, Item 5013 $17.95

Thoughts & Feelings, 3rd edition, Item 5105 $19.95

Call **toll free, 1-800-748-6273,** or log on to our online bookstore at **www.newharbinger.com** to order. Have your Visa or Mastercard number ready. Or send a check for the titles you want to New Harbinger Publications, Inc., 5674 Shattuck Ave., Oakland, CA 94609. Include $4.50 for the first book and 75¢ for each additional book, to cover shipping and handling. (California residents please include appropriate sales tax.) Allow two to five weeks for delivery.

Prices subject to change without notice.